Railway Monographs N

THE ROLLING RIVERS

The Saga of Maunsell's 2-6-4 Express Tank Locomotives

C.E.J. Fryer

Published by Platform 5 Publishing Ltd., Lydgate House, Lydgate Lane, Sheffield S10 5FH, England.

Printed in England by Echo Press, Echo House, Jubilee Drive, Belton Park, Loughborough, Leics., LE11 0XS.

ISBN 1 872524 39 7

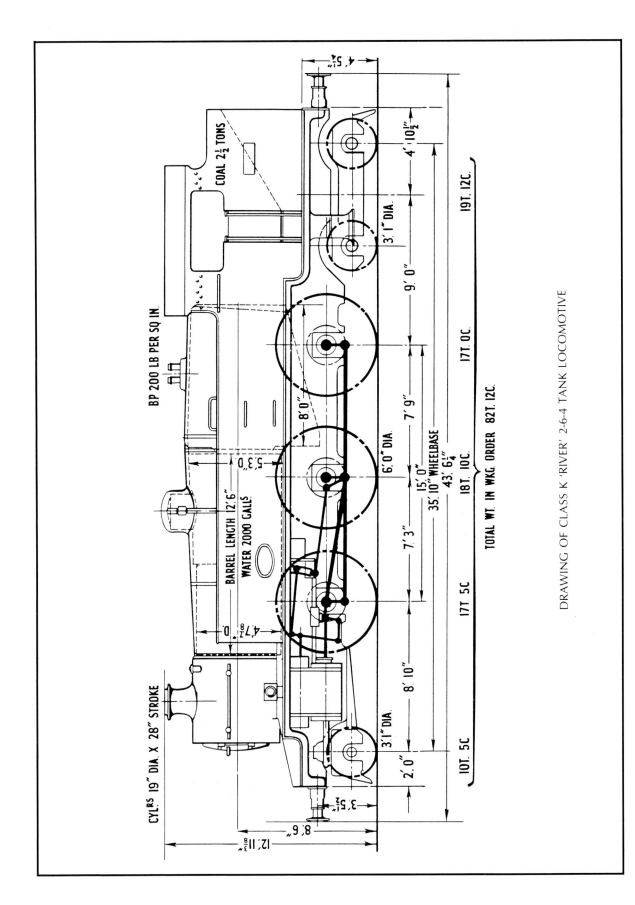

DRAWING OF CLASS K 'RIVER' 2-6-4 TANK LOCOMOTIVE

CONTENTS

Above: One of James Stirling's F class 4-4-0s, with 7 ft driving wheels, domeless boilers, cabs with typical Stirling-type wrap-over roofs, outside brake-rodding and springs outside the tender-sides. Of the 2 steam pumps ahead of the sand-box, one provides compressed air for the Westinghouse brakes, the other operates the reversing lever that controls the cut-off. These engines, dating from 1883, worked SER expresses for many years, but by the beginning of R.E.L. Maunsell's tenure of office at Ashford had mostly been relegated to minor duties. One, No. 240, was awarded a Gold Medal at the Paris Exhibition of 1889. *Courtesy: National Railway Museum Library: Chisholm Collection*

Below: A Stirling F class locomotive, No. 103, about to haul a two-van train loaded with locally-grown strawberries from Bexley to London, in the early 1900s. *Courtesy: Photomatic Ltd*

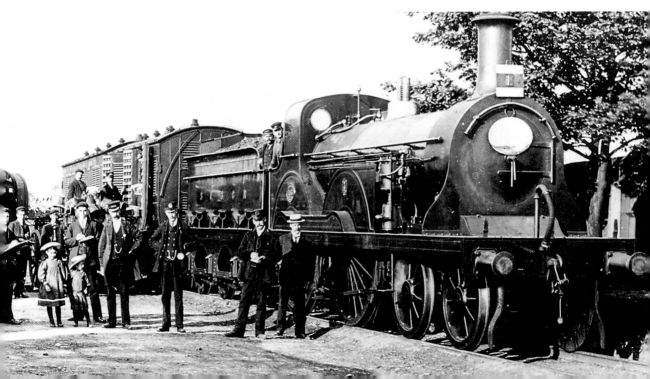

1. THE SOUTH EASTERN & CHATHAM RAILWAY 1899–1913

When I was a boy somebody presented me with a book, long since lost, to my great regret, about the railways of Great Britain. I cannot remember the title or the author's name, but it was published before the 1923 Grouping of the railways, and the larger main companies were dealt with in the order of their supposed 'greatness'. The London & North Western, self-styled The Premier Line, was placed first, the Great Western second and the Midland third; at the other end of the scale of valuation the South Eastern & Chatham came ninth, the Lancashire & Yorkshire tenth and the London Brighton & South Coast eleventh; the Scottish lines were then given separate consideration and Ireland was left right out of the picture. How these importance-levels were estimated it never occurred to me to enquire, but I was glad to know that the SECR was not in the lowest place, since it was peculiarly *my* railway. We lived at Tonbridge on its main line from 1915, when I was six months old, until 1927, and I had opportunities to watch, and occasionally to travel on the trains that passed through that interesting little town, which was still a community in its own right and not yet a dormitory for commuters to London. There were a few lineside stances behind iron railings or the parapets of brick over-bridges, which I frequented in my spare time. H.S. Wainwright's D and E class 4-4-0s and the older domeless engines of the same wheel-arrangement built by James Stirling were to be seen on semi-fast trains, on secondary duties or just shunting, and I became aware in some manner that the 'D's were locomotive aristocrats which had come down in the world; their handsome lines and proportions remained through their former gorgeous livery had vanished and they were now black and grimy after many years of wartime and post-war drudgery.

My championship of the SECR, which during my residence in Tonbridge became a part of the Southern Railway, in defence of which I used to stand up stoutly when the respective merits and demerits of the four chief systems were argued out at school, had this much to be said for it: in quite a number of respects the SECR was unique. No other railway had as many as four London terminal stations. No other line crossed the Thames by as many as four separate bridges. No other line had as many as 37 tunnels on its system, all within 80 miles of London. No other line catered for second-class passengers right up to the moment when it ceased to exist as a separate company. No other line linked London with the Continent through as many as four separate ports – Dover, Folkestone, Queenborough and Gravesend. To descend from the general to the particular, no other line had compartment doors on the insides of which notices in two languages warned passengers against putting their head out of the windows. *Ne pas se pencher au dehors* was the first French sentence I learned.

One might also add that no other railway had come into existence through the amalgamation of two bitter rivals into a single working partnership. It was not of course unknown for two contiguous railway systems to feel mutual animosity; one may instance the Caledonian and the Glasgow & South Western, or (for a while) the Highland and the Great North of Scotland. But the ill-will between the South Eastern and the London Chatham & Dover companies had been of long duration and was felt at its keenest in the reciprocated dislike between their Chairmen, Sir Edward Watkin and James Staats Forbes respectively, which had something of an 'Achilles-versus-Hector' quality. However, both gentlemen eventually disappeared from the scene, unmourned by their companies' shareholders, Watkin in 1984 and Forbes in 1898, and in the latter year both concerns, whose joint interests lay in co-operation rather than confrontation, agreed to act together in all matters while still remaining financially distinct.

When one examines a railway map of the south-east of England produced in the early years of the present century, one can see just how far competition, so often lauded as a necessary condition for successful business operation, had resulted in wasteful expenditure. Canterbury, Gravesend, Maidstone, Margate, Ramsgate, Whitstable, Ashford, Chatham, Dover, Rochester and Sevenoaks were all separately served by both railways, the first six also having different stations at the extremities of their different routes. Steamers between Dover and Calais competed until 1898 with those between Folkestone and Boulogne, each offering a service of approximately equal speed and convenience between London and Paris. The routes branching out from each main line's chief traffic artery into the territory of the other interlocked like the legs of two dogs fighting. The consequence was that when the working partnership of 1899 was at last achieved, Kent had more railway mileage for its size than any other county outside the London area, and after the 1923 grouping had taken place and both lines had become a part of the Southern system, quite a quantity of track was found to be redundant and was discarded, as also were some of the surplus stations.

The SECR after 1898 comprised two principal routes between London and Dover, that by way of Tonbridge, Ashford and Folkestone (itself as far as Tonbridge a shortening of the original route through Croydon and Redhill) and the rival route by way of Swanley, Chatham, Faversham and Canterbury. In the London suburban area there was an intricacy of loops and divergences,

SECR M1-637

Above: One of William Kirtley's M class 4-4-0s, built for the London Chatham & Dover Railway in 1881, with 6 ft 6 in coupled wheels, Westinghouse brakes, outside brake rodding and hand-operated reversing gear. Note the railway company's monogram on the tender side. In Kirtley's time LC&DR engines were liveried in black and always kept very clean. Note the warning bell on the tender which could be operated from within the train.

Courtesy: National Rail Museum Library

Below: A Stirling B class locomotive, No. 445, on the 3.45 pm Charing Cross to Hastings parlour car train, composed of Pullman-type saloon vehicles, near Grove Park, July 1914. Note the straight sides of the luxury vehicles, and the leading ordinary compartment coach with the 'birdcage' roof above the guard's compartment.

Courtesy: Locomotive Club of Great Britain: Ken Nunn Collection

Dartford being approached by three distinct routes; further from London there were many other branches, of which the line from Tunbridge Wells to Hastings, which continued east and north through Winchelsea and Rye to rejoin the main line at Ashford, and that from Faversham along the north cost of Kent to Margate and Ramsgate were the most important. Another former SER branch reached Canterbury from Ashford along the valley of Stour and continued to Ramsgate, meeting at Minster Junction the continuation of the main line to Folkestone and Dover which had followed the coast through Walmer, Deal and Sandwich. Yet another left Paddock Wood and traversed the Medway valley through Maidstone to Strood, where it met the continuation of the North Kent line through Dartford and Gravesend. The former LCDR also put out a branch from, Sittingbourne to the Isle of Sheppey and Sheerness, and dug deep into SER territory with another which diverged to the South from the main line at Swanley, followed the Darenth valley to Otford, turned east to cross the Medway at Maidstone and then continued South of the ridge of the North Downs to join the SER main line at Ashford; this route was to be particularly useful in later years as an alternative for London-bound boat trains. The SER also had a long westward extension which led from Tonbridge through Redhill and Guildford to Reading, invading the territories of the LBSCR, LSWR and GWR and making through running from the latter line possible, so that the towns of Kent could be reached from the north and west by a route which avoided London altogether. Besides these there were a number of other smaller branches, some of which have now been closed.

The newly-united companies between them controlled the shortest and quickest routes to the Continent by way of Dover and Folkestone, and the former SER route, the least difficult in regard to gradients, was the one which most boat trains followed. Just prior to the First World War there were six daily services each way, only the 11 am from Victoria, which stopped at Herne Hill to attach a through portion from Holborn Viaduct, taking the Chatham route, with the 5.20 pm up from Dover as its return working; all the others started from or ended at Charing Cross, calling at Cannon Street *en route* and then reversing, and then taking the main line by way of Tonbridge and Ashford. One service, the 2.20 pm from Charing Cross *via* Folkestone and Boulogne, reached the French capital in less than seven hours; even to-day one cannot do better than this unless one uses the Hovercraft service. (I am of course writing before the expected opening of the Channel Tunnel). Until 1910 there was also a twice-each-way service between Victoria and Queenborough Pier, Sheerness, connecting with a boat to or from the Dutch port of Vlissingen (horribly Anglicized in the timetable as *Flushing*) which took between 77 and 85 minutes for the 50 ½ miles, halting at Hearne Hill to attach or detach a Holborn Viaduct portion. In 1911 this service was transferred to Folkestone in order to shorten the sea-crossing and meet the competition from the Harwich – Hook of Holland route of the Great Eastern Railway steamers.

Neither the boat trains nor those that served the other large centres of population within the SECR's ambit were fast by the standards of the lines North of the Thames. This was partly because of the congested state of the lines in the south-east London area, where as yet there had been no electrification and trains trod on one another's tails, and partly because of the heavy gradients which had to be negotiated when crossing the North Downs and other hill ridges. Furthermore, until the union of 1898 the SER authorities had imposed a general maximum speed of 60 mph over their whole system. After the unification higher speeds were tolerated for a while over SER lines. The LCDR's expresses had in any case always been more sprightly downhill. In 1904 Charles Rous-Marten clocked 75 mph on a down Folkestone express near Hildenborough. However, the clutch of serious accidents which occurred on a number of other railways in 1906 through excessive speed over restricted sections of track brought about renewal of official discouragement, and for some years afterwards the mile-a-minute rate was seldom exceeded. Passengers were generally more interested in punctuality than in speed.

An examination of the 1910 timetable shows that the SECR drivers were not expected to be speed merchants. There was no start-to-stop timing as fast as 54 mph. On the former SER lines there was a handful of short-distance timings averaging between 53.7 and 51.1 mph. The fastest of the boat trains averaged 45.3 mph from Cannon Street to Dover. On the hilly line between Tonbridge and Hastings no start-to-stop timing reached 40 mph.

Throughout the period of its separate existence the SECR, apart from some through trains to or from the GWR main line, used non-corridor compartment stock on all its expresses except (from 1921 onwards) on its boat trains. It was not the only line to do this; the LBSCR followed the same practice even on through trains between London and Portsmouth. Refreshments were not therefore obtainable *en route* except from restaurants or platform trolleys when the train stopped at a principal station long enough for purchases to be made. Equally important, there were no on-train toilet facilities for third class passengers. Those travelling in other classes might be luckier. Users of Mr Wainwright's new coaches, brought out in the early 1900s, initially for the boat trains but later used in other trains as well, could always discover a lavatory compartment adjacent to where they sat if they travelled first class, and *might* find one if they travelled second class. The LBSCR did not go as far as this with their ordinary stock, but if one travelled in one of their first class Pullman cars one was doubly served, for the attendant could supply them with refreshments as well. However, in 1910 the SECR was not using such luxurious vehicles, though it had done so in the past and was to do so again once the First World War had ended.

For its main line passenger trains the SECR relied entirely, during this period, upon different varieties of 4-4-0s. During this time as Locomotive Superintendent on the SER James Stirling had built 88 Class F engines of this wheel arrangement, with 7 ft driving wheels and domeless boilers, to which he subsequently added 29

Class B engines, similar to the Fs but with slightly larger boilers. When the two companies united at the end of the century these were the principal passenger locomotives in use on the SER. The LCDR's last Locomotive Superintendent, William Kirtley, had built 44 of his M Class 4-4-0s, which came out in several batches from Longhedge Works, the final few not being completed till after the unification, so that they never bore LCDR numbers. They were slightly smaller and less powerful than Stirling's B class and were domed. To these, in 1900, were added six importations from Scotland, small-wheeled 4-4-0s designed by William Pickersgill for the Great North of Scotland Railway and built by Neilson of Glasgow, which being found to be surplus to the GNSR's requirements, were sold to the SECR to tide over a temporary shortage of locomotive power.

In 1901 the first of a series of newly-designed 4-4-0s appeared, which eventually totalled 51, some being built at Ashford Works, others by outside contractors. These were to be the mainstay of the company's express Services during the next decade. James Stirling had now

Left: Wainwright D class locomotive, No. 737, built in 1901, and restored at Ashford in 1960 for exhibition at the National Railway Museum.
Courtesy:
Kent County Library, Ashford

Below: Wainwright D class locomotive, No. 493, minus the polished brasswork in wartime grey at the head of a down train near Grove Park in 1918.
Courtesy: Photomatic Ltd

Wainwright E class loco-motive, No. 273, the first of its class, built in 1905. With slightly smaller coupled wheels and a Belpaire firebox, it was a trifle more powerful than the D class. Here it appears in photographic grey before receiving its Brunswick green and Indian red livery and having its brasswork polished.
Courtesy:
Locomotive Publishing Co

Wainwright E class loco-motive, No. 36 as later superheated and given an ex-tended smokebox; this proved so successful that many others were similarly modified. Note the double spectacle window on each side of the cab, to give improved forward visibility and the 'capuchon' on the chimney to improve the draughting.
Courtesy: National Railway Museum Library

Interior of Ashford Works in 1906. Note that all the workmen are wearing cloth caps except for one standing on his own - a foreman suppor-ting a bowler.
Courtesy: Kent County Library

retired, to be succeeded as Locomotive Superintendent by H.S Wainwright, son of a former Carriage and Wagon Superintendent on the SER, while Robert Surtees, who had been Kirtley's Chief Draughtsman at Longhedge Works, assumed the same position at Ashford, where locomotive and rolling-stock construction was now concentrated. It was in fact Surtees, not Wainwright, who master-minded the design of the new D class engines, though it was the latter who devised the new livery given to them, as to all other passenger engines on the railway, so that when in clean condition they were among the most magnificent objects to be viewed on any British railway. In their Brunswick green and red, with elaborate lining-out and polished brasswork, they were well calculated to impress foreign visitors to our shores as they left the gangway from the packet boat. Surtees's professional skills ensured that handsome was as handsome did; the new engines were equal to every task required of them until train loads began to increase at the end of the Edwardian decade, and were very free-running. A few years later a development of the D class followed, the E class, very similar in appearance to their predecessors except in having Belpaire fireboxes and slightly smaller driving wheels; they were also a trifle more powerful.

About 1910, however, increasing train loads forced the conviction that something more powerful still was needed. Wainwright at first thought of building a 4-6-0 type, such as McIntosh had introduced for express passenger work on the Caledonian main line in Scotland, and proposed two such engines in turn, one with inside, the other with outside cylinders. The Civil Engineer, however, considered they would be too heavy for the track, even though the weight on each pair of coupled wheels would have been less than 18 tons. So a 4-4-0 it had to be, and before Wainwright's retirement in 1913 the L class design had been prepared by Surtees.

and his staff. It was to have a larger boiler and firebox, larger cylinders and a superheater. It was left to Wainwright's successor to order these locomotives, of which more will be said in the following chapter.

Wainwright's tenure of the Locomotive Carriage and Wagon Superintendency at Ashford, to which was also added the supervision of the Locomotive Running Department, resembled the proverbial bright morning followed by clouds and rain. He had started well, tackling the difficulties attendant on managing a locomotive department constituted from the union of two rival lines, and which had included the transference of most of the building, repairing and maintenance operation, both with engines and rolling stock, from Longhedge to Ashford. He was well liked by those under him, but he had been given too much responsibility, and overwork together with a heart condition, began to affect his health. He had personal problems too. His wife had excessively expensive tastes in dress and jewellery which it was difficult to meet, and eventually she solved this problem to her own satisfaction by running away with a millionaire. Wainwright duly divorced her, but took the failure of his marriage hard. The grip he once had on his department lessened; methods of work at Ashford become slipshod; things went missing and nobody bothered to look for them; repairs and maintenance work fell into arrears; locomotive availability, efficiency and timekeeping suffered. The Board appreciated Wainwright's problems but things could not be allowed to go on in this way. In the end he was persuaded to resign on grounds of poor health and given quite a generous pension. He left Ashford at the end of November 1913 for the obscurity of retirement and died less than twelve years later at the age of sixty. A few of his locomotives, repainted in the livery he chose for them, remain as his memorial.

Wainwright's one attempt to build a tank locomotive for main line passenger trains on the Hastings branch, where gradients were very steep. The wheels were only 5 ft 6 in in diameter. Five were built but proved unsuccessful on the Tonbridge – Hastings line since they could not run fast enough downhill, so they were transferred to the London Bridge – Redhill section. Seen here in SR livery and re-numbered. *Courtesy: Photomatic Ltd*

2. ASHFORD WORKS UNDER NEW MANAGEMENT 1914

Wainwright's successor was a man of quite a different stamp, and only a few years his junior. Richard Edward Lloyd Maunsell was of Irish birth, had his schooling in Armagh and subsequently became a graduate of Trinity College, Dublin. It was not usual for railway engineers to have had a university education, and Maunsell's was the consequence of his father's insistence that he should take a degree in law, so that when he got over his youthful passion for engineering he would have a profession to fall back upon. He obtained the degree but persisted in the passion, and at the age of twenty went to Inchicore Works, Dublin, on the Great Southern & Western Railway, to serve for three years as a pupil under H.A. Ivatt while the latter was still Locomotive Superintendent there, having not yet gone to succeed Patrick Stirling at Doncaster. Maunsell next took himself to England and worked for a year on the Lancashire & Yorkshire Railway. In 1891 he was appointed as assistant Locomotive Superintendent on the East Indian Railway. Five years later he returned to Ireland as Works Manager at Inchicore.

Here he acquired a reputation for industry and thoroughness, both in play (he became a first-class cricketer) and work, and became noted for his refusal to tolerate irregularities - a trait to be seen later at Ashford. His subordinates regarded him as a 'terrible straight man.' An amusing tale was told of the alleged unauthorised use by the railway of the town's water supply at Athlone. A complaint was laid by the Town Council, that it had been surreptitiously tapped. This came to Maunsell's ears, and he took the matter seriously, though no one had expected him to, and ordered the pipe in question to be dug up and examined. The allegation was indeed found to be correct; a junction with the town's supply *had* been made at some remote date in the past; however, the connection was so clogged up by rust that it had obviously not functioned for many years. One would like to know the contents of the letter subsequently sent to the Town Council over Maunsell's signature.

His further promotion might well have been to the Great Northern Railway of England, to replace D.E. Marsh when the latter went to Brighton to be Locomotive Superintendent on the LBSCR in succession to R.J. Billinton. Ivatt remembered Maunsell's abilities, and pressed for him to be appointed as his Personal Assistant, but another man was selected. Had Maunsell gone to Doncaster, and had he and not H.N. Gresley thereafter been appointed to succeed Ivatt, the locomotive history of the LNER would have taken a very different turn - just what, one cannot imagine. However, in 1911 Robert Coey, the Chief at Inchicore, retired, and

Maunsell was appointed in his place as Locomotive Superintendent. He stayed in his post for a little over two years, scarcely long enough to make a mark on the Company's locomotive practice, though he did supervise the production of a number of 0-6-0 tank locomotives and a single very handsome express passenger 4-4-0, No. 341, *Sir William Goulding*. Both types were fitted with Schmidt superheaters - an innovation since all previous engines built at Inchicore had used saturated steam. The solitary 4-4-0 turned out to be a powerful and successful engine, but proved also rather too heavy for the track it had to run on; as is so often the case with locomotive singletons it did not have a long life, being withdrawn in 1928.

Maunsell's reputation for efficiency and thoroughness preceded him to England, where the SECR's Management Committee were anxious to straighten out the muddle into which things had fallen at Ashford. Wainwright, who had in any case had too much on his plate, being responsible for the daily performance and availability of the locomotives and rolling stock, as well as for producing and maintaining them, had been let-

R.E.L. Maunsell, Chief Mechanical Engineer of the South Eastern & Chatham Railway from January 1914, and subsequently of the Southern Railway.

Courtesy: National Railway Museum Library

L class 4-4-0 No. 770, one of 12 built by Beyer Peacock & Co. of Manchester in 1914, still in wartime livery in 1920, near Grove Park hauling a train of refurbished surburban 6-wheeled coaches.
Courtesy: Photomatic Ltd

ting the control of the works slip out of his hands into those of the Chief Clerk, Hugh McColl, a dour and rugged Scotsman who had gradually been building up an autocratic empire and running it with an iron hand, irrespective of the fact that much of what had to be done was beyond his proper competance. Someone, McColl seems to have felt, had to take a firm grip of things, and if Wainwright were content to let him do so, thus it should be. Aware of the situation, the Management Committee's Chairman, Sir Francis Dent, and his colleagues on the Board resolved to appoint in Wainwright's place a man of strong character who could impose his will on people like McColl (who was not yet due to retire) and do things *his* way. The other men in the top jobs at Ashford, Surtees in particular, *were* approaching retirement age, so it was hoped that confrontational situations could be avoided (as on the whole they were) and that the new broom at Ashford would be able to sweep clean with the help of some additional brooms whom he would be given a free hand to appoint.

Maunsell was selected in November 1913 and took up his duties the following January. A measure of the importance the SECR management attached to his appointment was seen in the salary he was to receive · £2,000 a year for the first twelve months, then rising to £2,500. (Wainwright had only been receiving £1,550 a year). His responsibilities were also lessened, that of locomotive running being transferred to another department under its own head. It was stated at the time that if all had been well at Ashford a younger man would probably have been chosen, but that it was felt necessary to obtain someone with experience in re-organization.

Two things needed to be done when Maunsell took over – one immediately, the other as soon as possible. The first need was for sufficient locomotive power to be able to work the train services when the summer traffic began. This meant new building without delay. As mentioned above, a design for a 4-4-0 had been prepared, but construction had not yet begun and Ashford Works was in no position to build the number needed in the short time available. Outside builders would have to be chosen. The immediate lack of locomotive power was met by the unusual expedient of hiring engines from other lines – a number of 2-4-0s from the GNR and some 0-6-0s from the Hull & Barnsley Railway – but more powerful machines than these were required for the expected summer traffic between London and the coastal resorts and ports of Kent and East Sussex and for the Continental Boat Trains. So the new L Class design had to be built speedily, but Maunsell, who did not yet know the design team at Ashford as well as he had known its counterpart at Inchicore, and who did not wish to buy a pig in a poke, decided first to send the drawings to be vetted at the latter place by his former Chief Draughtsman, W Joynt. The latter made a number of suggestions, including a shortening of the lap and valve-travel, which he thought were excessive as proposed.

Long-travel piston valves with long laps were part of the received orthodoxy at Swindon, but not yet in Dublin. Joynt's opinion might well have been sound in regard to locomotives having run on leisurely schedules

like those customary on the GSWR, but he was in effect recommending that Maunsell should build into his engine a hindrance to free running when on fully-open regulator and with a short cut-off. This was to be borne out later, though in the conditions which prevailed during 1914 – 1918, unforeseen at the time when the recommendation was made, high speed did not matter. Maunsell took Joynt's advice in regard to the valves, which was perhaps a pity; he also gave the cab a slightly larger roof with its rear end supported on pillars. As to getting the engines constructed, the only outside firm which would undertake to have some ready by the following June was A. Borsig of Berlin, who were given ten to build, the manufacture of a further twelve being undertaken by Beyer Peacock & Co of Manchester. The German-built ones were given Schmidt superheaters; the ones from Manchester had the pattern devised by J.G. Robinson on the Great Central. Later on Maunsell designed a superheater of his own, and the L Class engines were each fitted with one as it came in for heavy repairs during the thirties.

The immediate traffic problems was thus solved, at the cost of somewhat disgruntling the existing design team. However, Surtees was about to retire, so no grudges remained to be nursed at Ashford, where a thorough shake-up was impending. During the early months of 1914 Maunsell began to recruit new men for the principal positions at Ashford, and made six important appointments, of which the most critical was that of the new Chief Draughtsman, James Clayton, who came from the Midland Railway's works at Derby. Clayton had had a varied career. He had begun as an apprentice at Beyer Peacock's at Manchester, after which he went to Ashford and spent some time in the Drawing Office under Surtees. Subsequently he took a post in a motor-car manufacturing firm at Coventry to obtain experience in motor and transmission design with internal combustion engines. While here he came into contact with the brilliant if somewhat wayward Cecil Paget, who while Works Manager at Derby was devoting almost all his spare time to devising a new type of all-purpose six-coupled locomotive with rotary valves and as many as eight cylinders, which were arranged back to back and drove on all three coupled axles. This was Paget's own private interest, though he naturally hoped that after it had been built at his own expense the MR might take it up if, following tests, it proved to be successful. Having been completed, the engine developed faults while it was being tried out; these might conceivably have been overcome had the Company been more sympathetic, but Paget was regarded as a bit of a maverick and too clever by half, so the engine was put on one side, and eventually scrapped while its maker was in France on active service during the war. Clayton described this engine, and his own part in its design in an article in the *Railway Gazette* for 2nd November 1945. Paget eventually secured him a position at Derby, where he rose to be Assistant Chief Draughtsman. In recruiting him Maunsell secured someone with an open mind who was not afraid of new ideas, though he always retained a preference for Midland methods.

Of comparable importance to Clayton was G.H. Pearson, whom Maunsell appointed as Assistant Chief Mechanical Engineer and Works Manager. He had been at Swindon for many years, and had risen to become Carriage and Wagon Works Manager under G.J. Churchward, who was then probably the most prestigious locomotive engineer in the whole country. Pearson and Clayton were the ones Maunsell principally consulted in regard to locomotive design, so this meant that Swindon traditions as well as those of Derby would compete for influence at Ashford. It was Pearson who first suggested the building of large tank locomotives for working the express passenger services on the SECR - of which more below.

Other important appointments at this time were L. Lynes (from Swindon) as Chief Carriage and Wagon Draughtsman, C.J. Hicks (from Inchicore) as Pearson's assistant, H Tonkin (from Swindon) as Cost Accountant and H Holcroft (from Swindon) as Works Assistant with special responsibility for reorganizing the Works at Ashford. Lynes, Tonkin and Holcroft together with Pearson made up the ex-GWR element in the team to two-thirds, which ensured that design policy would come under the indirect influence of Churchward. In his Autobiography, *Locomotive Adventure*, Holcroft left a two-volume account of his years as one of the Maunsell team, during which he himself took a considerable part in designing locomotive details. It was due more to him than anyone else that the Southern Railway built a number of three-cylinder locomotives during the 'twenties and 'thirties. His account reflects the great respect he felt for Maunsell and the latter's developing aims and policies during the 24 years of his chieftaincy, first at Ashford, then at Waterloo.

By the middle of 1914 all looked set for considerable change in the Locomotive Department of the SECR. The latter had the potential to become a very successful and profitable railway. The proximity to London of the many seaside resorts which it served the growing practice of many people in the lower middle and working classes to take an annual seaside holiday, and the fact that the line offered the shortest route from London to Paris in terms of time, and to Belgium and Western Germany in terms of distance as well, all combined to promise an increase in traffic. In addition many businessmen were choosing to live at a distance from the capital and commute daily to work, even from as far away as Hastings.

Nobody in mid-1914 really expected the outbreak of a European War involving all the Great Powers. A series of crises in the Balkans had to all appearances been successfully overcome. The only quarter from which trouble seemed to threaten was across the Irish Sea. But the powder-kegs were there, and it only needed a large enough spark to light a succession of fuses. In Sarajevo, in Bosnia, on 28th June 1914, the assassination of the heir to the Austro-Hungarian Empire by a group of Nationalist fanatics began the sequence of events which led to the two rival power-groupings commencing hostilities. The British Declaration of War against Germany on 4th August, which was to disorganize the life of the whole nation as never before, gave the SECR a vital role to fulfil during the following four and a quarter years since it was the line that linked the rest of Great Britain with the Channel ports. More than any other railway in the country its operations for the duration of the War were governed by the obligation to convey troops, weapons and ammunition to be shipped to the Western Front. Maunsell and his team, and especially Maunsell, who was made Chief Engineer of the Railway Executive Committee which controlled the whole British railway system while hostilities were in progress, had little time in which to devise and carry out plans for the locomotive future of the SECR; their hands were full with other things. However, some discussions they did manage to have, and decisions were taken as to the provision of new engines which, even before the War ended, were translated into the manufacture of two prototypes which illustrated the intended locomotive policy on the line once peace gave the chance to pursue it.

L class 4-4-0 No. 777, one of ten built by Borsig of Berlin for the SE&CR and delivered just before war broke out. For 12 years these were the mainstay of the SE&CR's fast passenger services. They were good and reliable engines with loads up to 250 tons on the fastest schedules.

Courtesy: Kent County Library

3. PLANNING NEW LOCOMOTIVE TYPES

While the First World War lasted the first priority for the whole railway system in Great Britain was the furtherance of the war effort. This affected operations on other trunk lines by degrees, but on the SECR it controlled everything that happened right from the start. Here one unexpected task after another had to be coped with: the transporting into Britain of crowds of immigrant Belgian refugees driven from their homes by approaching enemy armies; the immediate requisitioning of the Company's cross-channel steamers by the Government for war purposes; the unfinished terminal station at Dover Marine having to cope with unexpected floods of traffic; the operation of troop trains one after the other, together with regular leave and ambulance trains, and the occasional running of special trains from London to convey important personages to the Western Front. All these together placed an enormous burden on the railway. Other lines North and West of London might continue to maintain existing schedules for a while, but the SECR could not afford the luxury of retaining an unaltered timetable. The new L Class 4-4-0s, intended for use on expresses, instead found themselves hauling trains of great weight at moderate speed. The locomotive department was stretched to its limits.

To make things worse, in December 1915 two falls of chalk from the cliff-face which rose steeply to the North of the line from Folkestone to Dover blocked the track between those towns and obliged all rail traffic to the latter town and harbour to follow the former LCDR route through Northern and North-Eastern Kent. It was still possible for people to travel by train on their lawful occasions within Kent and East Sussex, and no restrictions were laid upon movement into the area, as happened during the Second World War. It was even possible for civilians to cross into France by way of Folkestone and Boulogne. However, the taking of seaside holidays on the Kentish coast was over for the time being.

Ashford Railway workshops found themselves involved in a novel situation, being given the task of keeping going a great many Belgian locomotives, coaches, vans and wagons which had been withdrawn into Northern France in front of the advancing German armies during the first four weeks of the fighting, before the establishment of a more-or-less static front and the formation of trench lines between the Flemish coast and the Vosges. The replacement of parts for this rolling stock had to be carried out at Ashford, the nearest place where facilities existed. Spares were not available, so the replacement parts had to be specially machined after the faulty ones had been examined and measured, there being no drawings available. This was a priority task,

since the Allied Front had to be supplied from the rear through the French railway system, many of those workshops were now behind enemy lines. One small component which had become worn out or damaged could put a whole engine, coach, van or wagon out of use until a replacement could be fitted. The workshops and drawing office at Ashford had to manage as best they could, and for some jobs special tools had to be obtained.

Despite these distractions, and the need for Maunsell to be frequently away from Ashford to meet and consult with other members of the Railway Executive Committee, the expected peace-time needs of the SECR were not lost sight of. Until fairly late in the course of the War it was taken for granted that all the railway companies would return to their former status and be independent concerns again, and plans for a new locomotive policy were made on that basis, both in regard to freight and passenger trains.

The SECR, unlike the larger lines North of the Thames, did not have heavy freight flows between the London area and the other large conurbations in the south-east, but it did have some, and in contrast to the West Coast, East Coast and Midland main lines it had no long stretches of quadrupled track to enable goods trains to keep out of the way of expresses. There was traffic in commodities between the capital and the sizeable towns on the company's system, of which towns sixteen were fairly large and eight rather smaller, despite the fact that Kent in those days was a mainly rural county. There was also some interchange of freight traffic with the Continent, and the East Kent coalfield also added its quota. In consequence Ashford became a marshalling focus for the eastern end of the county, while Hither Green served the same purpose near London, the main freight flows moving between them in either direction. It would have been much easier to organise these movements if the line between those places had been similarly graded throughout, but while between Ashford and Tonbridge, through the Weald of Kent, the going was relatively easy, there were some tough inclines between Tonbridge and Hither Green. Paddock Wood, itself conveniently linked with Maidstone and the Chatham area by the line along the Medway valley, accordingly became an intermediate marshalling point where a long train could be divided into two shorter ones which could be taken up on the banks on either side of Knockholt summit. In the other direction the opposite process took place. With stronger locomotive power these operations could be simplified and single trains be taken through without division.

At the beginning of the century Wainwright had produced his C Class 0-6-0 freight engines, which were sound and reliable but lacked the pulling power to cope with the steeper parts of the line when the loads were sizeable. Their nominal tractive effort was under 20,000 lb. The tougher pitches between London and Tonbridge, which included short stretches at 1 in 120 North of Knockholt and six continuous miles mostly at the same gradient and partly in tunnel between Tonbridge and Sevenoaks, were beyond their unaided powers with trains of any weight, so double-heading or rear banking had often to be employed. D.L. Bradley, in his monograph *The Locomotives of the South Eastern & Chatham Railway* recounts how, during the First World War,

> . . . . an important duty often entrusted to Cs. . . . was the Gunpowder Specials from Plumstead sidings to Richborough . . . . when running *via* Tonbridge these trains were worked in two parts to St. Johns, where reversal took place. Then one of the engines banked from the rear as the other tackled the combined train from the front. At Knockholt summit the banker shut off steam and dropped back to return home light engine. Water was also taken at Tonbridge, and it took skilful manipulation of the engine and van brakes to halt these heavy and highly dangerous trains at the water crane. The Tonbridge Fire Brigade was always turned out and paraded on the station platform, complete with horse-drawn steam pump, when such specials were expected, a supply of water being kept in one of the Urban District Council's water carts in the station approach.

Eventually the explosives arrived at the coast by way of Ashford, Canterbury and Minster Junction and were shipped across the Channel from the temporary wartime port of Richborough at the mouth of the Stour.

Something more powerful than the C Class 0-6-0 would be needed when normal traffic was restored and the uneconomic use of two engines, allowable in wartime conditions, could no longer be tolerated. The Cs were weak in ability to pull largely because their boiler pressure was as low as 160 lb per square inch, so a stronger boiler was indicated, which would also require to be more capacious to supply the steam to larger cylinders. The whole locomotive would therefore need to be heavier and an additional pair of wheels would be needed to carry the extra weight. A 2-8-0 wheel arrangement was considered, but ruled out because it was felt that the new type ought to be available for use on semi-fast and excursion trains, so that they could be assigned to useful diagrams and not be obliged to stand idle for long periods. It was assumed that too many coupled wheels would hinder free running. (One wonders what Maunsell would have thought if he had been able to foresee the British Railways' Class 9F standard 2-10-0, which more than once proved its ability to reach 90 mph with passenger expresses, despite having coupled wheels of only 5 ft diameter.) Eventually a 2-6-0 wheel arrangement was decided on.

In regard to passenger trains the problem was somewhat different. An engine was needed which could haul loads considerably heavier than had been customary in Wainwright's time, at somewhat higher average speeds, and which would at the same time have

a high route availability. All this was in the context of main routes which in places were heavily graded. It was also intended to follow a standardisation policy, so that as many as possible of the new 2-6-0's components should be interchangeable with those on passenger engines. Wainwright, observing the tendency for loads to increase, had, as already noticed, considered building 4-6-0s for use on the heavier passenger trains, but the Civil Engineer had turned the idea down. He had also experimented with tank locomotives - in one case deliberately, in the other under pressure from the Management Board.

Early in 1913 he built five 0-6-4 tank engines, of the J Class, having in mind the haulage of the morning and evening business trains between London, Tunbridge Wells and Hastings. Because of the very severe gradients south of Tonbridge he gave the new locomotives coupled wheels of only 5 ft 6 in in diameter. They were something of an experiment and, so as far as the Hastings road was concerned, by no means a success, for while they could certainly surmount the banks without difficulty they could not develop sufficient speed on the level and downhill in order to keep time. They were eventually transferred to work between London Bridge and Redhill by way of Croydon.

At about the same time the SECR had the offer of some 4-6-4 tank engines which had been built by R.H.Whitelegg for the London Tilbury & Southend Railway. Even before these had been built the MR took the LT&SR over in 1912, and at Derby it was decided that these large engines were not really needed. One of them was loaned to the SECR and ran trials on different parts of its system. The SECR's Management Committee was keen to obtain them, but Wainwright and Surtees, who had made a point of riding on their footplates, would not agree, maintaining that they ran unsteadily, and their veto was accepted.

In face of these two experiments it may seem surprising that Pearson should have proposed to Maunsell that the new passenger type should be a tank locomotive, and that the latter should have accepted the suggestion. It seems the more surprising when both must have known that L. Billinton's new 4-6-4 express tank locomotive *Charles C. MacRae* had shown itself to be unstable as originally designed and had needed the insertion of well-tanks between the frames to hold most of the water supply -something which Maunsell and Pearson do not appear to have contemplated. It seems possible that Pearson had in mind the GWR's 4-4-2 'County tanks', version of Churchward's 4-4-0 'County' Class express passenger tender locomotives, which were coping very successfully with the faster outer suburban trains from and to Paddington. He suggested that all the SECR's expresses might eventually be operated by six-coupled tank engines, with the exception of the boat trains, for which it was intended to use Victoria instead of Charing Cross as their London terminus so as to avoid the traffic congestion between Hither Green and London Bridge. (The approach line from Bickley Junction to Victoria was part of the original LCDR system, on which a number of the over-bridges were not at that time considered strong enough to cope with heavy wheel-loadings. On the other parts of the main line system six coupled engines were now acceptable).

However, the question was whether a tank engine could carry sufficient coal and water for a 70-mile non-stop run. In regard to coal, while this was a commodity which could not so easily be loaded on to a locomotive as water, yet if it were of good enough quality (a very moot point on the SECR which largely relied on coal from the East Kent collieries, which was not as good as some of the best coal available in the Midlands or South Wales) a bunker of 2½ tons' capacity would seem large enough. For such a quantity to be completely used up on an 80 mile run, the consumption would need to be almost 70 lb a mile, much more than was customary even on heavy trains. Given that the bunker was full at the start of the journey there should be no difficulty on this score. But water was a different matter. On the LBSCR six-coupled tank engines had been or were being constructed for service on fast trains, while Marsh had already built 4-4-2 tank engines, some of which had successfully run the fiunny South Express' day in and day out between Rugby and Croydon by way of Kensington and Clapham Junction, some 90 miles, without running short of water. The longest non-stop run regularly being performed on this line was over the 51 miles from Victoria to Brighton, but longer runs with only brief stops, in which there was not enough time to re-fill tanks, were also being successfully managed by the above-mentioned 4-6-2s and 4-6-4s. If the Victoria to Portsmouth journey, which included several stiff banks, could be accomplished by engines that did not incorporate the latest front-end improvements based on Swindon practice, which the Ashford design team had in mind, then a similar distance without the need to re-fill could surely be achieved by an engine with side tanks of a nearly-equal capacity which *did* have these improvements.

Side tanks, however, have two disadvantages compared with tenders. In the first place they tend to hamper the driver's forward view along the side of the boiler, and so for that reason cannot be made too high. Secondly, when a large part of the water within them has been consumed, what is left tends to swish from one side to the other, which may cause the engine to roll. This tendency can be mitigated by placing baffle-plates inside the tanks, but this of course slightly lessens their capacity.

One method of overcoming the water-shortage problems would have been to lay down water-troughs, as had been done on all the main lines North of the Thames and on the GWR. During his superintendency Wainwright had considered having this done, and the main routes in the SECR system had been carefully inspected, but only one suitable site had been found, near Headcorn between Tonbridge and Ashford. Only a few trains would have found troughs sited here of benefit; they would not have served those which ran on the former LCDR line or on the Tonbridge-Hastings section. It was therefore not thought worth the expense of putting troughs here, together with the necessary water-softening plant, as well as of equipping a sufficient number of locomotive tenders with water pick-up apparatus. Maunsell and his team concurred with this decision so far as the immediate future was concerned, though the eventual installation of troughs was envisaged. As regarded tender locomotives, the LSWR had shown that large 8-wheeled tenders could hold enough water for the 108 miles' journey from Waterloo to Bournemouth to be made without a stop, and if need be the SECR could construct such tenders (though this was never done).

Eventually it was decided to build a single prototype of each of the two Classes: a 2-6-0 tender locomotive for mixed traffic and freight work, with 5 ft 6 in wheels, and a 2-6-4 tank engine for express passenger work, and then to evaluate them by seeing how they shaped up to the work they were expected to do.

4. THE PROTOTYPE K CLASS EXPRESS TANK LOCOMOTIVE

On June 18th 1917 the first of the new design of passenger tank locomotives, No. 790, emerged from Ashford Works, having been completed two months before its mixed-traffic counterpart, the N Class 2-6-0 No. 810, which it much resembled. Both together, in the words of D.L. Bradley,

> . . . . . proved to be the most outstanding locomotives constructed for service in this country since the pioneer work of Churchward between 1903 and 1907

Much of the description which follows is true of both types, which differed only in the sizes of their coupled wheels so far as the machinery and steam-providing components were concerned.

To deal first with the boiler and firebox: both were larger than on any SECR locomotive so far built, and had features reminiscent of Swindon practice. The boiler, like the 'Standard No. 4' used on the GWR's celebrated 'City' 4-4-0s, was tapered on its second ring and of similar maximum and minimum diameter, but over a foot longer. (Seen from the outside the tapering appeared to be continuous from smokebox to firebox, the boiler cladding being so shaped.) It reached its highest point just above the furnace throatplate. The steam space above the firebox, which was one of the Belpaire type, had an upper roof which sloped slightly downwards towards the cab, and the firebox sides were similarly-sloped inwards towards the rear. The highest point for the collection of steam for the cylinders was, as in Churchward's locomotives, above the front edge of the inner firebox, and here a transversely-set perforated steam collector pipe was situated, instead of in the dome, which latter was a cover for the top-feed system. It was placed near the front end of the tapered boiler ring, and corresponded with the distinctively-shaped brass bonnet on Churchwards's locomotives, but whereas the latter included the safety valve Maunsell's dome served merely to house the water-admission apparatus. A pair of safety valves, of the 'Ross Pop' type, were set above the firebox about 2 feet in front of the cab. Two feed-pipes, each half-embracing the boiler on either side as in GWR practice since 1910, carried the feed water from the injectors to the dome on either side, within which it fell on to a tray which sloped spirally downwards · known colloquially by those who had to fit or service it as the 'helter skelter lighthouse'. Trickling down this tray, it was warmed by the surrounding steam before falling into the boiler water below. This arrangement was somewhat different from that in a Churchward engine, where the feed water fell on to perforated plates and dripped through their holes; this was satisfactory enough when suitably soft water was available, but it was otherwise in chalky South-Eastern England, where perforations would soon have become blocked up. It was found in practice that Maunsell's spiral trays collected deposited chemicals in the form of a fine powder which could easily be cleaned off when the engine was serviced. The working steam pressure was 200 lb per square inch, 40 lb greater than that of the L Class engines.

The superheater, designed by Maunsell, was a modification of the type used at Swindon, having three tiers of elements instead of two. The principal of superheating, as first developed by Schmidt in Germany and then modified by other locomotive engineers, is that steam from the boiler, instead of being taken straight to the cylinders in a state of saturation, was instead passed along tubes looped back and forwards upon themselves, each collection of loops being within a larger tubular flue carrying hot gases from the firebox to the smokebox. This extra heating raised the temperature of the steam, so that it did not readily condense within the cylinders (which, should it occur, might damage the latter, since water is virtually incompressible and, if trapped between the cylinder head and the moving piston coming to the end of its stroke, might burst the cylinder open). The hotter steam, charged with extra energy, could work against the pistons to give a greater pressure upon them – or alternatively the same force with a smaller cut-off. Thus fuel and water consumption could be lessened. Churchward's practice had been to employ only moderate superheat, enough to dry the steam and prevent water-deposition in the cylinders, but other locomotive engineers found that it was advantageous to supply a greater degree of superheat than Churchward did, so long as the lubricating oil with which the steam came into contact was not broken down in consequence of being subjected to higher temperatures.

Maunsell conformed to Churchward's practice, both in the prototype K Class 2-6-4 tank engine and its fellow N Class 2-6-0, giving each 100 square feet of superheating area less than had been given to the L Class 4-4-0s. Later, However, when adding to the numbers of each class he increased the degree of superheat considerably by extending the looped pipes within their flues. The steam, both before and after being superheated, passed into and out from separate spaces in a cast-iron chamber, the 'header' in the smokebox, and from there was directed to the steam chest, the piston valves and the cylinders. Maunsell's design of the header permitted the easy removal of the elements for cleaning or repair; they could be taken out and put back easily, one at a time.

The cylinders were outside the frames – another

Above: The first K class passenger tank engine, No. 790, built at Ashford in 1917, intended for fast passenger trains in the SE&CR. In many respects it was a complete departure from previous Ashford practice, more particularly in having 2 outside cylinders, outside Walschaerts valve gear, a coned boiler, top-feed apparatus inside the dome, a superheater of Maunsell's design, a boiler pressure as high as 200 lbs. p.s.i., cab-styling modelled on Derby usage, and a leading 2-wheeled truck.
Courtesy: National Railway Museum Library

Below: A front right-hand view of K class tank No. 790 at Ashford soon after its construction. The man in the Homburg hat is probably R.E.L. Maunsell.
Courtesy: Kent County Library

break with SECR usage, inside cylinders having been the rule since the two constituent lines had begun operation in the mid-nineteenth century. Piston valves were employed instead of slide valves, and were directly above the cylinders and so easy of access. Maunsell's rule, was wherever possible, to 'make everything get-at-able', a principle observed later when the BR standard types were designed, so that fitters and repairers would not need to do so much standing in pits beneath the engines or contort their bodies to reach beneath the boiler with spanners or wrenches. With outside cylinders, motion and valve gear, almost all the moving parts and their bearings were accessible from one side or another of the locomotive. The cylinders had prominent piston tail rods whose sheaths pointed forwards from the centres of the cylinder covers; these helped to support the sliding piston rods but were later judged to be unnecessary. They were never removed from the K Class before their eventual rebuilding, but in process of time most of the N Class 2-6-0s lost theirs. At the rear of each cylinder a single slide bar supported the cross-head; this was believed at the time to be sufficient, but experience later dictated the addition of a second one, as described in the following chapter.

Walschaert's valve gear was used, a type not previously fitted to any SECR engine and still comparatively rare in Great Britain, where the most commonly-used gear was the Stephenson type, which was not so well-suited to outside-cylinder designs with piston valves above the cylinders (though the GWR used it in nearly all their engines, employing rocking bars when necessary to operate valve spindles outside the frames) since it involved the placing of eccentrics on the driving axle, two to each valve. It was heavy compared with Walschaert's gear, in which the necessary movement was imparted to each valve spindle partly by a lever taking its movement from the crosshead, and in part from a rod attached to a sliding block in a curved slotted lever that was rocked to and fro about a central pivot by another rod from a crank outside the connecting rod big end. In regard to the length of valve travel, Maunsell did not repeat the error he had made with the L Class 4-4-0s, but gave it a full 6½ inches, ¼ inch longer than Churchward was giving his latest '4300 Class' 2-6-0s, in order to permit the freest possible passage to the steam as it entered or was exhausted from the cylinder.

As to the storage of coal and water; the former, as already indicated, would be sufficiently supplied from a bunker of 2½ tons' capacity. The water supply required long side tanks holding 2,000 gallons in all. One wonders whether it may have crossed the minds of those in the design team, that such large side tanks might render the locomotive unstable when running. They had the Hassocks derailment on the LBSCR before their eyes. But equally they knew that the same line had been using tank engines for fast express running since 1908 without untoward incidents. A tank engine was presumably stable enough on a well-maintained track;

this seemed to be the lesson of the LBSCR and GWR 4-4-2 tanks. There seems not at this stage to have been any suspicion that the SECR main express routes might have patches of faulty track, or that maintenance once wartime conditions had ended would not be entirely satisfactory.

The locomotive's smokebox and chimney were strongly reminiscent of contemporary Derby practice, as also was the cab with its rounded-off roof edges. Right-hand drive was employed. The regulator lever in the cab controlled the admission of steam not in the dome, as was customary, but within the smokebox next to the superheater header. The valve gear was adjusted by means of a screw wheel with projecting handles.

The coupled wheels, at 6 ft diameter, were only 6 inches larger than those of the N Class 2-6-0. Apart from the J Class 0-6-4 tank engines already mentioned, built by Wainwright four years earlier, no other locomotive intended for express passenger service on the Kentish lines had been given coupled wheels as small as this. However, it was reckoned that since all the main routes between London and the Kentish and East Sussex coasts included steep gradients · very steep on the Tonbridge to Hastings stretch · a six-foot diameter would be the most advantageous. Good hill-climbing would matter more than an ability to run fast level or downhill grades. The coupled wheels were given steam brakes, which sufficed for the whole engine.

An innovation was the employment of a two-wheeled Bissel truck in place of a leading bogie. This had its anchorpin attached to a cross-stretcher between the frames some distance to the rear of the truck's axle, the weight of the front of the engine being taken by a bearing of the Cartazi slide type. The theory behind this device was that the weight of the engine itself operated to return a truck or bogie to its central position. The heavy mass of the locomotive's front end bore first upon a hemispherical casting resting on a similarly-shaped hollow depression; below that a V-shaped bearing lay upon a similarly-shaped support. Movement of the bogie or truck sideways slid one or the other side of the V-bearing to left or right against the force of the weight above it. By building up the sides of the lower bearing an oil-well was formed so that the sliding surfaces were effectively lubricated.

Externally the engine looked drab even when new. Maunsell had adopted as a wartime economy measure for all the SECR engines a grey paint which was not only cheaper to apply than the former lined-out livery, but also contained a chemical resisting rust and corrosion. This livery, if such it may be termed, remained standard during the four years following the end of the War. Only after the Southern Railway was formed was it changed to the more acceptable lined-out dark green. The number 790 was painted in large white numerals on each tank side, and the ownership was indicated by a small plate on the side of each bunker, lettered 'SECR'.

5. TESTING AND MULTIPLYING THE PROTOTYPE

Like many other locomotive engineers, Maunsell preferred, when putting an entirely new type of locomotive on the rails, to test it for a lengthy period before multiplying its numbers. In the case of his largest engine, the four-cylinder 4-6-0 *Lord Nelson*, built in 1926, it was to be almost two years before further members of the Class began to appear. In the case of the N Class mixed-traffic 2-6-0 he waited a full two years before ordering more to be constructed, and by then Ashford Works had become so disorganised by wartime requirements, and the backlog of other necessary work was so great, that it was the middle of 1920 before the second of its type entered service. Four more followed at approximately six-weekly intervals, and the supply then slowed down considerably, the tenth not appearing before December 1923. By this time the SECR had been a part of the Southern Railway for almost a year, and Maunsell himself had become its Chief Mechanical Engineer, supervising the production of locomotives not only at Ashford but also at Brighton and Eastleigh. Since the N Class appeared in slow succession one might have expected the K Class of 2-6-4s more or less to have matched them, but in fact No. 790 remained the solitary example until the beginning of 1925, which needs to be explained.

As already mentioned, it had been decided during the War years that, when hostilities had ended, all Continental boat trains should originate from or terminate at Victoria instead of Charing Cross or Cannon Street, so that they could use the less-congested approach over the former LCDR metals through Penge and Bickley. The largest locomotives which the Civil Engineer would allow to be used over this section were the original E Class 4-4-0s, the superheated ones, pending the time when the weak over-bridges could be strengthened. The two superheated Es and the L Class were considered too heavy, and, of course, the single K 2-6-4 was much too heavy. So the L Class 4-4-0s, which would have been used on boat trains had they been running from or to Charing Cross, were available in their entirety to work the other expresses, and to have built several new 2-6-4s would merely have made perfectly good 4-4-0s redundant. The prototype No. 790 was enough to be going on with, and it could be tried and tested at leisure. Since nearly all its parts were interchangeable with the corresponding parts of the N Class 2-6-0s, and since these were needed for freight traffic, it was better to concentrate on producing *them*. Had there not been a War things would no doubt have been different; the weak bridges would have been strengthened more expeditiously and the Ks would have been built in large

numbers more quickly.

It was a full six years before orders were placed for more 2-6-4s. During that time the prototype was very thoroughly tested out. Once it had been run in on local trains between Ashford and Tonbridge or Canterbury it was given a special trial over the 70 miles of main line between Cannon Street and Folkestone, principally to discover if it could carry sufficient water in its tanks for a journey of that length with a load much greater than the maximum then envisaged for a fast express. On 23rd August 1917 the 1.40 pm from Charing Cross to Folkestone was made up to 340 tons, and No. 790, on an easy wartime schedule of 102 minutes, covered the distance in less than booked time despite a number of severe checks *en route*. This was encouraging, but rather less so was the fact that a mere 150 gallons of water remained in the tanks on arrival at Folkestone. The engine clearly did not have the hoped-for reserve capacity. The immediate consequence was that it was shedded at Tonbridge for a while to work over the 29½ miles between that station and the capital, on which short stretch there would be no risk of the tanks running dry. Then, in October 1917, it was transferred to Bricklayer's Arms shed and put under the care of one driver, who could become acquainted with it and get to know its peculiarities.

From then until the spring of 1922 it worked on a regular daily diagram which included one lengthy non-stop run, as follows:

1. 3.40 am newspaper train, Cannon Street to Ashford, stopping at London Bridge, Sevenoaks, Tonbridge and Paddock Wood, arriving at Ashford at 5.27 am and then running light to Folkestone.
2. 8.10 am up business train, Folkestone to Cannon Street, stopping only at Sandling Junction and London Bridge and arriving at 9.40 am. This required a level of performance almost equal to that of the later crack 80-minute expresses as some time had to be allowed for the two stops.
3. 4.36 pm semi-fast, Cannon Street to Tonbridge, stopping at London Bridge, Sevenoaks and Hildenborough and arriving at 5.28 pm - a much more leisurely assignment.
4. 7.36 pm slow from Tonbridge to Cannon Street, calling at all stations and arriving at 9.01 pm.

One may remark that if the same driver were expected to work the whole diagram he would never have got a decent night's sleep.

As might have been expected, the most difficult stage of the daily four was the second. The train included, latterly, a Pullman car, and would usually have weighed some 220 – 230 tons empty, considerably less than

Above: One of the batch of 9 K class tank locomotives built by Armstrong Whitworth & Co. of Newcastle and delivered early in 1925. They matched the prototype No. 790 in almost all respects, and were named after rivers on the SR system. The locomotive shown is No. A 794 'River Rother', in lined green SR livery. No. 790 now became A 790 and was similarly liveried and named 'River Avon'. *Courtesy: Kent County Library*

Below: A right-hand view of No. A 794 'River Rother'. The Westinghouse brake steam pump, visible beside the smokebox, was fitted to all the 9 Armstrong Whitworth engines, since this brake was used on the Central Section, where this batch was first put to work. *Courtesy: Kent County Library*

on the occasion of the test run noticed above; in spite of this there were occasions when the water supply looked like running short and an unscheduled stop for replenishment had to be made at Tonbridge. Apart from that the engine was a success and no difficulties were experienced in keeping time, nor were there any complaints from the footplate staff about the way it rode - none, at any rate, that were set down in writing.

In the autumn of 1922, on Maunsell's instructions a series of comparative tests was carried out, in which No. 790 competed with two 4-4-0s, one an L Class engine, the other a rebuilt D, over the main line from Ashford to London and back. Each locomotive did a spell on a particular pair of trains, the 8.39 am from Ashford to Cannon Street and the 3 pm from Charing Cross in the return direction. The timings were not demanding: 24 minutes for the 21.3 miles from Ashford to Paddock Wood, 9 minutes thence over the 5.3 miles to Tonbridge, 15 minutes for the 7.4 miles onwards to Sevenoaks (up steep gradients almost the whole way) and 30 minutes for the 20.2 miles thence to London Bridge. In the other direction 32 minutes were allowed to Sevenoaks, 12 from there to Tonbridge and 32 for the 26.8 miles on to Ashford. It was not in any sense a speed contest, but rather an attempt to discover whether the newer engine showed any advantage over the other two in economy of working. The loads varied between 232 and 243 tons empty.

Somewhat surprisingly the L showed up as well as the K when allowance was made for the fact that the former was pulling a loaded tender and the latter was not. Harold Holcroft, one of Maunsell's team of six at Ashford, travelled on the footplate on each occasion with all three engines. His estimate of the relative abilities of the L and K engines was that the former had the more efficient boiler, the latter the more efficient cylinders, and that overall there was practically no difference. One wonders what the results might have been if the loads had been increased or the schedules quickened. With their relatively short valve travel the Ls were not free-running engines, and if required to pull hard and fast did so best with a somewhat high cut-off and the regulator only partly opened - a method which certainly did not use the steam's expansive power in the manner approved at Swindon or, as things now were, at Ashford. As to the K, Holcroft had some interesting comments to make in his autobiography:

Locomotive Adventure:

> I had some trips on No. 790 . . . . It was very smooth-riding and had a most comfortable cab. If, however, it encountered a low rail-joint or a soft spot on the road it would give a heavy roll, followed by others of diminishing amplitude. These were accompanied by an unpleasant feeling of side-slip, possibly due to movement on the Cartazzi slides of the end trucks.

In view of subsequent events Holcroft's experiences might well be considered prophetic.

The tests appeared to show that the older locomotive was as good as the newer one, which was not exactly what had been expected, but it was nevertheless decided to go ahead and build more Ks. The parts for them, excluding the boilers (which were constructed by the North

British Locomotive Company at Glasgow) were produced at Ashford, and Armstrong Whitworth & Co of Newcastle-on-Tyne assembled the first nine and delivered them early in 1925. A year later Brighton Works, whose commitments were not as heavy as Ashford's built another ten. It was decided to give names to the whole sequence – a practice which the SR had begun with the 4-6-0 'King Arthurs' and which was continued with all express engines subsequently built for service on it, with the exception of the 15 L1 Class 4-4-0s constructed in 1926 to supplement the existing Ls.

There were certain differences between the newer engines and the prototype. The front Bissel truck of No. 790 had helical springs, but those of all the later 2-6-4s had laminated springs. Each cross-head was given a second set of slide bars. Maunsell had taken a calculated risk when deciding that one was enough, both in the 2-6-0s and the 2-6-4s, and early reports had seemed to bear out his opinion that undue wear would not ensue, but he evidently altered his mind when it became evident that ash and grit thrown up from below were causing the single bars to become abraded, so a second bar was added on each side to give increased support to the cross-head and to act as a shield against such intrusions. The third change was greatly to increase the degree of superheat to more than a third as much again; here he was profiting by the experience of locomotive engineers on other lines, that high superheat brought further benefits over and above the obviating of condensation in the cylinders. A fourth alteration was to admit steam from the boiler to the superheater header from the top of the inside of the dome instead of from a perforated pipe above the front of the firebox, and to place the regulator there, a break with the Churchward pattern hitherto followed. In later designs of locomotive the 'helter skelter lighthouse' top feed also disappeared, and the dome became what it had been before, a point for the collection of steam where its transmission to the cylinders was regulated, and nothing more.

By the end of 1926 all twenty 2-cylinder K Class engines had been completed and named after rivers which flowed through SR territory. Meanwhile a further 2-6-4 tank had joined them, which had three cylinders in place of the other two, and which at the front end looked externally distinctly different. This production of an 'odd one out' among the Ks seems to have been in large part the consequence of a piece of personal enterprise on Holcroft's part. He was a champion of the superiority, other things being equal, of three cylinder as against two cylinder propulsion in locomotives. While still at Swindon he had built a model in which he showed that the valve movements of a third inside cylinder could be successfully derived from those of two outside cylinders, and had brought it to Churchward's notice. The latter had been favourably impressed and had insisted that a patent should be taken out, though he himself was not proposing to build any three-cylinder engines (nor did he ever do so) and, so far as Swindon was concerned, the project got no further. After Holcroft had joined the SECR he was confined for a while to duties which did not include the designing of locomotives, but in 1916 an enforced absence from work

Above: No. A 796 'River Stour' on the turntable at Brighton. There was in strict necessity no need to turn these engines, but this was always done where the facilities existed.   *Courtesy: Kent County Library*

Below: One of the second batch of 10 K class tank locomotives, built at Brighton and put into service on the Eastern Section of the SE&CR (the former SE&CR). As will be noted, no Westinghouse brake pumps were needed on these engines as the Eastern Section used the vacuum brake. This locomotive was A 801 'River Darenth'. Note the way the rivets on the buffer beam stand out, the cleaner having left a layer of dirt around each river-head. *Courtesy, Lens of Sutton*

through illness gave him the chance to apply his mind again to the design of a derived valve gear, and he made another model which he showed to Maunsell, who was interested and asked many questions. However, the times then were not propitious for locomotive experimentation, and for the moment nothing came of it.

When the War was almost over H.N. Gresley, Chief Mechanical Engineer on the Great Northern, built a three-cylinder locomotive in which the inside cylinder was tilted so that the connecting rod could work a crank on the second coupled axle without fouling the first. He had devised a derived gear of his own to operate the inside valve, in which the motion, as in Holcroft's two models, was derived from the motion of the other two valve spindles. The design of the engine occasioned some criticism from other locomotive engineers since, in order to bring all the valve spindles into the same plane, Gresley had tilted the outside cylinders also. Holcroft wrote to the *Engineer* outlining a method by which the outside cylinders could be brought back to the horizontal position, while at the same time a simple form of derived valve gear could be used on the inner tilted cylinder. At a later date he read a paper on the subject at a meeting of the Institution of Locomotive Engineers, and its contents came to Gresley's notice. The latter invited Holcroft to come and see him, and then told him that his suggestion had given him a clue to making a simpler derived gear for all his future three-cylinder engines. He also dropped a strong hint to Holcroft that he should leave Ashford and join him at Doncaster.

Holcroft loyally reported all this to Maunsell, who received the information without comment. However, it is evident that the latter resented Gresley's apparent attempt to detach from the Ashford team one of its most ingenious members, and a somewhat heated interview appears to have ensued between the CMEs. The upshot was that a week after Holcroft's disclosure Maunsell told him, 'I have seen Gresley myself, and have told him that I propose to construct some three-cylinder engines myself, and shall need your assistance here.' It is not clear how long Maunsell had been meditating such an intention, or whether indeed it was a ploy to continue to retain a good man's services. Holcroft was delighted at the prospect of being able to occupy himself with locomotive design again, and he began to apply his mind again to the details of a derived valve gear suited to the new type of standard 2-6-0 and 2-6-4 engines, so that the three-cylinder variants could be constructed.

It may be wondered why a derived valve gear should be thought so desirable. Could not the inside cylinder simply be provided with an additional Walschaert's gear of its own? The objection to this was the increased weight and the need to install machinery which was not easily accessible - an eccentric on the driving axle plus all the needful bars, bearings, rodding and sliding link apparatus. In their two-cylinder state these engines were already quite heavy. A little extra weight, however, could be tolerated because of a three-cylinder locomotive's more even torque, six impulses instead of four being given to the driving axle during each revolution. Part of this extra weight would be that of the more complicated cylinder castings, the rest in the levers, rods and pivots needed with a derived valve gear. Holcroft set himself to plan a system in which the derived gear would be light as possible. Originally he had thought of placing it to the rear of the cylinders, but as his ideas took shape he saw the advantage of bringing as many of the moving parts as possible round the outside and to the front of the cylinders where, in Maunsell's phrase, they would 'be get-at-able.'

When No. 822, the three-cylinder prototype of the N1 Class of 2-6-0s took to the rails in December 1922, the first thing an observer would have noticed as being unusual was the inward and upward slope of each outside cylinder, the inclination being to allow a long rod worked from the rear of the valve spindle to pass outside the valve chest and operate a system of levers immediately behind the front of the running plate; this was raised quite high, the descent to the buffer beam being not, as with the other 2-6-0s, in a curve above the leading wheels, but directly in a vertical plane. While this detracted from the engine's appearance it made for easier accessibility to the components of the derived gear.

The first N1 2-6-0 to have three cylinders was also the last locomotive to be built for the SECR, and the corresponding K1 2-6-4, made on the same principle, did not appear for another three years, coming out in December 1925. Unlike all the other Ks except the prototype it was wholly constructed at Ashford. Like No. 822 it had Holcroft's derived gear for the inside cylinder, and the front of the running plate was raised even higher above the outside cylinders, so that the final descent to the buffer beam resembled a vertical rock-face. This was necessary as the outside cylinders had to be higher above rail-level than in the N1 because the coupled wheels were 6 ft, not 5 ft in across. The boiler and smokebox were similarly pitched higher to allow for the rotation of the inside driving crank, so that it was necessary to fit a shorter chimney. Beneath the smokebox was the cylinder casting made in two parts, one including the inside cylinder, both bolted together. The side tanks also differed somewhat from those on the Ks, the gap at the lower front end of each being very much larger than the small oval opening on the two-cylinder engines. Beneath it was rather unsightly ladder with three footsteps just outside the front coupled axle. Invisible from outside, the crank axle had webs to act as counterweights so that it was not necessary to alter the cast-in counterweighting on the wheels; the same castings could therefore be used for making the latter as for those on the two-cylinder engines.

The locomotive entered service in December 1925, being numbered out of sequence with the others as No. A 890. It was put to work on the Eastern Section and for a while used on the 6 pm express from Cannon Street to Dover. It proved to have the edge over the two-cylinder Ks in regard to pulling power and free running, but was also slightly less stable, as the chapter next but one to this will show.

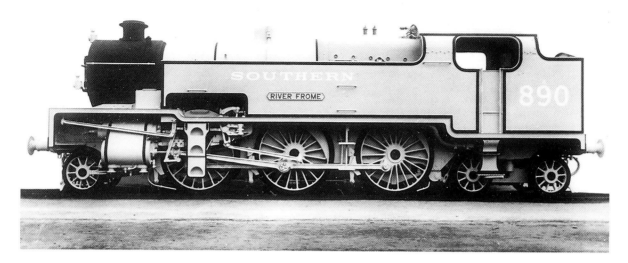

Above: No. A 890 'River Frome' the solitary example of a 3-cylinder K class tank engine, built in 1925. It has H. Holcroft's patent derived valve gear for the inside cylinder, worked form the outside cross-heads through forward-directed rods and rocking levers close to the buffer beam, which certainly detracted from the engine's good appearance. The engine is shown here in photographic grey immediately after construction. *Courtesy: Photomatic Ltd*

Below: Front right-hand view of No. A 890 'River Frome', with the vertical fall to the buffer beam prominent; behind it were the rocking levers that operated the inside valve motion. The oblong container in front of the tank is the sand-box for the front coupled wheel. The orifice in the tank side is wider than the similarly-placed one in a 2-cylinder K since it was necessary to reach the motion of the inside cylinder to oil it. *Courtesy: Photomatic Ltd*

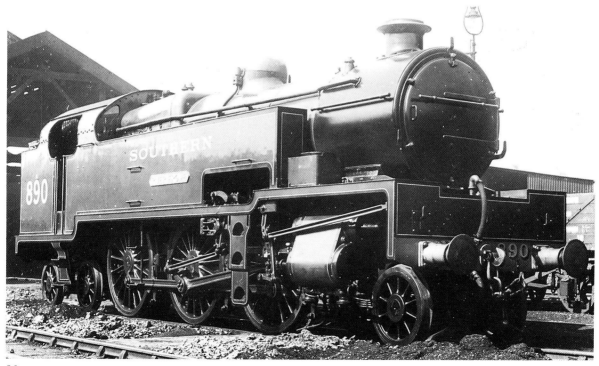

6. K CLASS 2–6–4s IN SERVICE 1925–1927

When the first production K 2-6-4s began to enter service the situation had greatly changed from what it had been when the prototype was built. The SECR had now ceased to exist. Locomotives were now available for use on the Eastern Section which could be drawn from other parts of the whole Southern system. Maunsell no longer had to think solely in terms of the former SECR's requirements; he and his staff had now moved from Ashford to Waterloo and were responsible for supplying locomotive power for trains running as far South as the Isle of Wight and as far West as Padstow in Cornwall. Expresses on the Kentish lines could be hauled by engines which had formerly worked from Waterloo; rebuilt Drummond 4-4-0s were beginning to be drafted there. A new era was beginning to dawn.

Had there been no grouping of railways in 1923, no doubt the 'tank engines only for fast passenger trains' policy would have been implemented, and a much larger number of Ks would have been built more quickly once the weak bridges on the former Chatham section had been strengthened. Quite possibly water troughs would have been installed in one or two places and some engines adapted to use them, in which case it might even have been feasible to reduce the capacity of the side tanks of the Ks and (though this would have been counter to the accepted standardisation policy) give them larger boilers. They might then have been employed on the boat trains. But these are mere speculations; absorption into the SR system was now a *fait accompli*. Rather one has to ask: should the prototype 2-6-4 have been multiplied at all? It is perhaps significant that when Nos. 791 – 799 first took the road they went straight to the Central section. The Eastern Section, it appeared, could make do without them.

It had occurred to Maunsell that the Ks would be very suitable for using on the fast trains of the Central Section, where a number of sixty-minute timings between London and Brighton had now re-appeared - in particular the twice-each-way journeys of the *Southern Belle* all-Pullman train and the *City Limited* business service to and from London Bridge. L. Billinton, the last locomotive Superintendent on the LBSCR, had constructed a handful of 4-6-4 'Baltic' tank locomotives to cope with these prestige trains. Their dimensions were greater than those of the K Class in almost every respect; their cylinders were 3 inches larger in diameter; they had 162 square feet more heating surface and nearly twice as much superheat; their grate area was larger; they had 3 ¾ tons more adhesion; they could carry a ton more coal; they had a much greater water capacity, having not only side tanks but well tanks, even though the depth of water in the former was restricted to 15 inches.

However, the Ks had the advantage of a higher boiler pressure, 200 instead of '70 lb per square inch, and they also had a more up-to-date front end design. It seems to have been as much the Brighton line as the Eastern Section that Maunsell had in mind when he decided to multiply the prototype. If his somewhat smaller and lighter engines, weighing 15 ¾ tons less than the 'Baltics', could do the job as well as the latter, there would be no need to increase the numbers of the 4-6-4s or to modernise them.

He therefore had the nine newly-built Ks and the original prototype fitted with Westinghouse brake apparatus for working on the Central section, sent No. 790 there ahead of the others to try out its paces between London and Eastbourne, and then, when all ten had been in service on that Section for a few months, arranged for a series of comparative trials in which No. 792 *River Arun*, was matched against Baltic No. 331. Each was given the same pair of trains to run - the 11.05 am up from Brighton and the 3.05 pm down *Southern Belle* from Victoria, for three consecutive days. Special coal, of which samples were sent for analysis, was reserved for both engines, and arrangements were made to record carefully the amount used by either. The engines were worked by their regular crew. Although it was not exactly a case of David being pitched against Goliath, the advantage certainly lay with the lighter engine - and indeed more so than was known at the time, for it was later found that No. 792 had a small leak in its boiler. As the tables of logs set out below show, the 2-6-4 proved to be the better performer. Holcroft travelled on each occasion and his timings were given to the nearest quarter-minute.

In each instance the 2-6-4 tank made the better showing, despite the fact that on the first and third runs signal checks were encountered, and that on the first run the train was a coach heavier than usual. It is a pity that Holcroft did not time to the nearest second, as then some estimate of speeds might have been made.

The up runs were all made when a permanent way slack was in operation at Coulsdon; signal checks also hampered progress in every case beyond Croydon, so that on no occasion was time kept. The runs may best be compared by observing progress as far as Coulsdon. Again, the K made the better showing, with slightly heavier trains, though the 4-6-4 made the faster starts from Brighton.

One is fortunate also to have a single log of a journey on the Central Section, on an Eastbourne express between Victoria and Lewes, which Cecil J Allen published in the *Railway Magazine* early in 1926. He had timed the train himself and wrote quite enthusiastically about

DOWN JOURNEYS:

Locomotive:	792	792	792	331	331	331
Load in tons (empty):	274	242	242	240	240	223
Date (Oct 1925):	13	14	15	20	21	22
Miles:	m. s.	m. s.	m. s.	m. s.	m. s.	m. s.
0.0 VICTORIA	00 00	00 00	00 00	00 00	00 00	00 00
2.7 Clapham Jn.	05 45	05 30	05 30	05 15	05 15	05 15
4.7 Balham	08 30	08 00	08 00	08 00	08 00	08 00
8.7 Thornton Heath	13 15	12 45	12 45	13 15	13 00	13 15
10.5 East Croydon	15 30	15 00	15 00 sigs.	15 45	15 30	15 45
12.7 Purley Oaks	18 00	17 15	17 15	18 15	8 00	18 15
15.4 Coulsdon	20 45	20 00	20 45	21 30	21 15	21 30
21.9 Earlswood	28 30	27 30	29 00	29 15	29 15	29 15
25.8 Horley	32 00 sigs.	31 00	33 15	33 00	33 00	33 00
29.5 Three Bridges	35 45	34 00	37 00	36 45	36 45	36 45
34.1 Balcombe	41 45	38 45	42 00	42 00	42 00	41 45
38.0 Hayward's Heath	45 15	42 15	45 15	45 45	45 45	45 15
43.8 Hassocks	50 30	45 00	50 00	51 15	51 00	50 45
49.5 Preston Park	56 45	53 15	55 45 sigs	57 45	57 00	56 45
50.9 BRIGHTON	59 45	56 45	59 00	60 00	59 15	59 00

UP JOURNEYS:

Locomotive:	792	792	792	331	331	331
Load in tons (empty):	217	215	214	187	202	201
Date (Oct 1925):	13	14	15	20	21	22
Miles:	m. s.	m. s.	m. s.	m. s.	m. s.	m. s.
00.0 BRIGHTON	00 00	00 00	00 00	00 00	00 00	00 00
01.4 Preston Park	03 30	04 00	03 45	03 15	03 15	03 00
07.1 Hassocks	10 30	11 30	11 15	10 15	10 30	10 15
12.9 Hayward's Heath	15 30	16 45	16 15	15 45	16 00	15 45
16.8 Balcombe	19 15	20 30	20 15	20 00	20 00	19 45
21.4 Three Bridges	23 45	25 15 sigs.	24 45	24 45	24 45	24 45
25.1 Horley	26 45	28 30	27 45	28 00	27 45	28 00
29.0 Earlswood	30 30 sigs. PWS.	34 15 PWS.	31 45 sigs. PWS.	32 00 PWS.	32 00 PWS.	32 00 PWS.
35.5 Coulsdon	38 45	43 45	39 30	40 00	39 45	39 45
38.2 Purley Oaks	42 45	47 45	43 15 sigs.	42 45	42 45 sigs.	42 45
40.4 East Croydon	45 15	50 15	45 30	45 00	45 15	45 00
42.2 Thornton Heath	47 45	52 30	48 15	47 00 sigs.	47 30 sigs.	47 00
46.2 Balham	52 45	57 00	52 45	52 15	54 15	51 30
48.2 Clapham Jn.	55 00 sigs.	59 00 sigs.	55 00 sigs.	60 00	59 00	53 45 sigs.
50.9 VICTORIA	61 00	64 30	60 15	67 00	65 30	60 15

No. 799 *River Test*, resting between duties during its period of use on the Central Section. Note the prominrent Westinghouse brake apparatus above the right-hand cylinder, needed on the Central Section, but removed later when it was transferred to the Eastern Section. Cecil J. Allen recorded a run behind this engine on a Victoria – Eastbourne train, and wrote of it appreciatively – see below.
Courtesy, Lens of Sutton

the engine's performance. His description and log appear below.

"Let me mention a brilliant run on the Brighton section behind one of Mr Maunsell's 'River' Class 2-6-4 tanks. They have not quite the same reserve of power as the Brighton 4-6-4 tanks as is only natural in view of their more limited dimensions, but given reasonable loads the 'Rivers' are exceedingly speedy engines, as my run amply proves. All the relevant details are given in the brief table. The train was the 3.15 pm down Eastbourne, the engine No. 799, *River Test*, and the load a 41-axle train of 250 tons gross. Delay was caused in the early stages by our having to take the local road from Croydon to Coulsdon, together with a couple of signal checks but from Quarry we went like the wind, touching 75 an hour at Horley and 74 at Hayward's Heath (we should have another 75 here but for sighting adverse signals before Wivelsfield) with an intermediate minimum rate of 53 at Balcombe Tunnel. We gained in fact three minutes from Coulsdon to Keymer. With all checks the gross time to Lewes was only 65 minutes 35 seconds, and unchecked I do not fancy we should have taken more than 62 minutes, although allowed 65 minutes".

These two maxima in the middle seventies appear to be the highest *recorded* speeds behind a K Class tank during the brief period when they worked express trains.

The second production batch, built at Brighton, were first run on the coast line to Portsmouth and then transferred to work on the westward extension of the former SECR between Redhill and Reading, where their six-coupled wheels were very useful on the many heavy gradients. One of them had the regular duty of hauling the daily through corridor train from Birkenhead, Birmingham and Oxford on the GWR line between Reading and Redhill in both directions.

The first batch of 'Rivers' remained in service on the

Locomotive: 2-6-4T No. A 799 *River Test.*
Load: 236 tons empty, 250 tons full.

Miles		Sched. m.	Actual m. s.	Speed mph.
00.0	VICTORIA	0	00 00	
02.7	Clapham Junction		06 50	
04.9	Balham	9	09 55	37 ½
06.8	Streatham Common		12 20	52 ½
09.4	Selhurst		15 55	46
			sigs.	
10.5	East Croydon	17	18 00	
13.6	Purley		23 00	41
			sigs.	
15.0	Coulsdon	23	25 50	
17.0	Star Lane Box		28 55	41 ½
18.8	Quarry Box		31 15	42 ½
21.9	Earlswood	32	34 15	70 ½
26.0	Horley		37 40	75
29.6	Three Bridges	40	41 05	60
31.9	Balcombe Tunnel		43 45	53
34.1	Balcombe		46 00	65
38.0	Hayward's Heath	49	49 25	74
			Sigs.	30
41.2	Keymer Junction	53	52 55	30
44.8	Plumpton		58 50	55 ½ /52 ½
47.7	Cooksbridge		61 55	60
50.2	LEWES	65	65 35	

Central section until early 1927, when a number of newly-built 'King Arthurs' were brought in to replace them; thereafter five of them joined their fellows on the Eastern Section, some being stationed at Ashford and Dover while five remained at Eastbourne. The former worked on trains to and from London by way of Tonbridge or Maidstone. Of their performances on this section no records seem to exist, which is not altogether

No. A 800 'River Cray', on a semi-fast train near St. Mary Cray. The train appears to be moving very slowly as the smoke and steam from the chimney are blowing forwards, not to the rear. The men in the cess at the side of the track, and the single sleeper in the 6-foot way, suggest a slowing for track repairs. This locomotive was the one involved in the Sevenoaks accident, which resulted in all the K class being converted to tender engines.

Courtesy: National Railway Museum Library: F.E. Box Collection

No. 792 *River Avon*, about to back onto a London-bound train at Brighton on a summer afternoon in 1925. This is the engine which, tested in trials the following October against one of Billinton's 4-6-4 tanks, proved somewhat better in performance despite its somewhat smaller size.
Courtesy, Lens of Sutton

surprising as they were there for only a few months before being taken out of service for reasons which appear later. However, we do have records of the 'odd one out', the three-cylinder No. A 890, *River Frome*, which was completed at the end of 1925, since Holcroft had a special interest in it. In the second volume of his autobiography he gave details of some journeys he made on its footplate.

The first of these, on 13th April 1926, was on the mid-morning train from Charing Cross to Dover, scheduled in 43 minutes between London and Tonbridge, where three coaches were detached; 33 minutes were then allowed to Ashford, another 23 to Folkestone Central and a further 17 to Dover, stopping at Folkestone Junction. The whole run was booked in two hours from London Bridge; the timing was certainly leisurely and the interest lies in the first part of the journey. With a train of 287 tons as far as Tonbridge a late start gave an opportunity to regain time. By the latter station 3¼ minutes had been picked up, two of them on the steep rise from New Cross to Knockholt. From Tonbridge onwards gradual time recovery continued, despite overtime spent at that station and at Ashford. For most of the journey the regulator was fully open and the cut-off early.

The second run, made on the same day with the same locomotive, was the return by way of Maidstone with stops at Folkestone, Sandling Junction and Maidstone East. Time was gained on the two longer sections but signal checks spoiled the conclusion of the run. On the uphill stretches, some of which had very steep banks, the regulator was kept fully open and the cut-off well back. However, the load was light and the engine never needed to be extended.

Holcroft's final footplate run an No. A 890 was with the 6 pm from Cannon Street to Ashford, which stopped at Sevenoaks and Tonbridge. The load was 255 tons tare and about 275 gross, as this was a commuters' train and well filled. The locomotive was hampered at the start by the fact that the fire had not properly burned through, so that the boiler pressure was only 150 lb per square inch all the way to Sevenoaks. Nevertheless time would have been kept had it not been for a momentary signal stop outside the latter station. The stop at Tonbridge platform allowed the pressure to rise, since the fire was now in good order, and a late start of one minute was easily regained on the subsequent stretch to Ashford, the 26.7 miles being covered in 29 minutes, with the regulator fully opened and the cut-off adjusted to suit the gradient in the best Swindon fashion. Of this part of his footplate journey, Holcroft wrote with much appreciation:

"It was my last and most memorable trip with No. A 890 and as perfect as possible. The shovelling plate on the bunker and the firedoor were on a level, and so spaced that the fireman could do his work by a swing of his body without lifting a foot. That, combined with the beautifully smooth riding, resulted in a total absence of spilled coal on the floor, and the cab was dustless. Steam pressure and water level were well up, and with the regulator fully opened and cut-off close to mid-gear the exhaust was inaudible. The engine seemed to skim along with the greatest of ease under the restraint exercised; the 26½ miles were reeled off in 29 minutes start to stop against a gently-rising gradient. It was a most pleasurable ride, and my feelings of satisfaction were enhanced by a proprietary interest in the engine, since I had been allowed a free hand in the designing of those parts which distinguished the three-cylinder arrangement from that of the two-cylinder".

All indeed seemed set fair for the 'Rivers' to have a long and useful career. But even as Holcroft was enthusing over No. A 890 fate was knocking at the door, since two-and-a-half weeks earlier this very engine had disgraced itself by coming off the rails near Wrotham in the first of a series of mishaps to K Class tanks which eventually spelt their doom.

7. FORESHADOWINGS OF CATASTROPHE

When Nos. A 791 – 799, the first production of K Class 2-6-4s began work on the Central Section of the SR they proved themselves, as already seen, perfectly capable of doing the work of the seven ex-LBSCR 4-6-4 tank despite being some 15 tons lighter. Cecil J Allen's log, reproduced in the previous chapter, demonstrates their ability in day-to-day service. It would also seem that no official reports were ever made that they rode unsatisfactorily. This is not, of course, to say that no verbal complaints were ever made on this score. According to D.L. Bradley, 'the Rivers' were not liked by the Central Section footplate crews, who did not appreciate their marked tendency to roll heavily and unexpectedly on indifferent track, and consequently refused to run them at high speeds'. But, as Allen's log indicates, this was not always the case. Drivers of steam locomotives always tended to be professionally conservative, and many of the Central Section men no doubt disliked having a product of Ashford Works foisted on them, but evidently the main line southwards from London was not considered 'indifferent track' and there were not many opportunities for running really fast on other parts of the Section. If the tendency to roll had been frequently felt, no doubt written reports would have taken the place of occasional grumbles, but we have Maunsell's word for it, made before an Inspector of the Ministry of Transport, that 'no complaints were received with regard to engines Nos. 791 – 799 during the one-and-a-half years or more when they were employed upon the Brighton Section and no restriction in respect of speed was placed on them'. It has also to be observed that at no time subsequent to this period were any adverse comments made about any of these nine engines.

However, the prototype, No A 790, now named *River Avon*, did have riding trouble reported in April 1925 when it was working trains on the Tadworth branch to Tattenham Corner, which was not a section where high speeds would be attempted. No doubt the track was 'indifferent' compared with that on the main line to Brighton; it was also a fact that the engine was now almost eight years old and a good deal of general wear and tear had occurred. It was accordingly taken in for examination and certain alterations were made. The centres of the front Bissel truck and rear bogie were made flat instead of hemispherical; both were given laminated springs for their wheels in place of the helical ones previously fitted, and the side-steadying springs of the front truck had their centres set further apart. Back in service, No. A 790 ran over a year and a half without any further unfavourable reports being made. The same modifications were intended for Nos. A 791 – 799 and for the three-cylinder engine No. A 890, but only the

latter was in fact modified, and then only by having the centres of the truck and bogie made flat. When the second batch, Nos A 800 – 809, were constructed, on the other hand, all three modifications were included. So, on the face of it, it should have been this batch which caused less trouble than the first; in fact it was the other way round, which rather suggests that the tendency to roll was not primarily due to the design of the engine but to some extraneous cause or causes.

When the construction of the second batch was complete, and all had been allocated to sheds on the Eastern Section, reports began to come in about undue rolling. Four locomotives were concerned, Nos. A 800, 801, 803 and 807, all of which had been built with the modifications described above. The complaints were made between March and June 1927, and the locations where the trouble occurred were widely spread over the Eastern Section: Cheriton Junction near Folkestone, Buckland Junction North of Dover Priory, Headcorn and Tudeley on the straight stretch between Ashford and Tonbridge, Maidstone and Wrotham on the Ashford-Swanley loop line, and near Reading. They were dealt with by sending the engines concerned to either Ashford or Brighton for examination. Three of the cases concerned parts of the main line where the track was relatively or absolutely straight, where any oscillation in the engine would not be expected to originate in its own mechanism – again suggesting that the cause was not in the engine, though a readiness to react to the cause might well be greater in a tank locomotive which carried out most of its water on either side of the boiler.

In this respect the experience of the LBSCR many years earlier seems to be relevant. After the first 4-6-4, No. 327 *Charles C MacRae*, had been constructed it displayed a tendency to roll, and on one occasion, at Hassocks on the main line to Brighton, while travelling at speed all six coupled wheels came off the track, though the wheels on both bogies remained in position. A little later, after the second 4-6-4 No, 328, was built, the same thing happened to *it*, this time at Fishbourne between Chichester and Portsmouth. In consequence it was decided to lower the centre of gravity by building well-tanks beneath the boiler barrel and between the frames, and this was done with both locomotives and their five successors. In actual daily operation, it was the well-tanks that held nearly all the water, the side tanks only being permitted to contain up to 15 inches' depth. The outside tank covers were retained, nevertheless, for what one may term cosmetic reasons; the engines would certainly have looked very strange if these had only been some eighteen inches high. But this reconstruction brought potential disadvantages, since if the well-tanks needed attention during maintenance it might be necessary to remove the boiler from the frame in order to get at them. It does not appear that Maunsell and his team ever considered reconstructing the twenty Ks in this manner; had the idea ever surfaced in discussion it would no doubt have been rejected as going against the policy of making everything get-at-able. In any case no such alteration could have been made to No. A 890, whose inside crank and motion occupied the space where such a well-tank would have had to be placed.

It was the latter engine whose misfortunes began the sequence of troubles that afflicted the type in 1927. On 31st March *River Frome* was derailed while heading an up train on the Ashford-Swanley Junction line between Wrotham and Otford. This occurred on a right-hand 39-chain curve when the speed was about 60 mph. A roll to the left caused the flange of the right-hand front coupled wheel to rise above rail level, come down on top of the right-hand rail, run along it for over 11 feet and then come down on the wrong side. Still moving forwards, the flange again mounted the rail, ran along the top of it for 27 feet and again fell down on the wrong side. Some distance further on there was a level crossing, and here the engine re-railed itself when the wheel was forced upwards by the road surface, which was of course at the same level as the top of the rail. The driver meanwhile had been conscious of the rolling but not of the derailment, and had applied the engine's brakes to check it.

An enquiry was held into this mishap, which brought to the light the poor state of the permanent way at this point. The derailment had begun at a place where the line passed through a cutting; drainage at such a site was always difficult since water could not escape sideways but only in the direction of the slope of the track-bed, and after a period of heavy rain (as was the case on this occasion) the site was sodden and the base of the track beneath the ballast was becoming deformed. As to the ballast itself, this was a mixture of shingle and sand.

Some comment seems appropriate here. Shingle was easily obtainable in Kent, more so than in any other part of the United Kingdom, as anyone who has visited its beaches will appreciate. The Dungeness area in particular held enormous quantities of it, driven up by the English Channel by the tides over hundreds of years. The disadvantage of using local shingle was of course the fact that the stones had been rounded by the action of the sea, and did not grip upon one another as granite chips or fragments of broken slag, such as other railway companies used, would do. A stablising ingredient had therefore to be added if shingle was employed on a railway track-bed. Sometimes sand was used, sometimes ash.

The SR authorities were by now well aware that the previous reliance upon shingle made for unsatisfactory support for the rails, especially when considerable loads were run over them (one remembers the long trains of Army tanks destined for the Western Front during 1917 and 1918) and broken Kentish ragstone was now replacing shingle, but wholly to carry this out over the entire system was a long job, and while some parts of the Swanley-Ashford stretch had been re-laid in this manner, others had not. The section where the derailment had occurred had been re-laid in 1905 with rails weighing 85½ lb per yard – not quite up to the main line standard, but the line from Swanley to Ashford had then been regarded as a branch over which fast running would not take place. The curve in question was supposed to have a super-elevation on the outer rail of 3 inches, but when it was measured after the accident it was found to have dropped by ½ inch. Speeds above 60 mph were not advisable over this patch, and a general 60 mph limit was imposed on the 'Rivers' and all other locomotives using the Swanley – Ashford line once the former were allowed back on to it the following July.

From the enquiry it appeared that *River Frome*, though the heaviest of the 'Rivers', was not responsible for the derailment, though it was possible that the driver may unintentionally have been partly responsible, since he applied the engine's steam brakes instead of braking the wheels of the train behind him when he first realised that the engine was beginning to roll. The latter method of braking hindered the forward motion of the engine without making the driving wheels bind in the vertical slides of the horn-plates, stopping them from moving up and down, something that application of the steam brakes alone might bring. The whole incident ended with a decision to bring the track up to main line standard as quickly as possible, since it was already being used as an alternative route for London-bound boat trains, and until that had been accomplished heavy locomotives, such as the Ks and the *King Arthur* 4-6-0s, were limited to a maximum of 60 mph when using it.

The next derailment happened on 2nd August, and was the result of No. A 800, *River Cray*, being allowed to traverse a curve in the sidings at Maidstone East, where it should not have been allowed to run. It derailed completely. It was an awkwardness rather than an accident; re-railing was successfully accomplished and the engine appeared to have been totally undamaged by what had happened to it. This may have been an illusion, since the shock of the derailing could have affected the springing. However, no re-weighing of the engine was done to see if this might be so. It was not a serious oversight, as ordinary running during the following two weeks would have shown if the wheels were not properly balanced, and evidently nothing amiss was observed. However, the incident could not fail to be raised later after this same engine was involved in a much more serious calamity. In any case, the design of the engine could have had nothing to do with the mishap; it had no business to be on such a sharp curve.

A third derailment took place on 20th August and again No. A 890 was the victim. At the head of a down train, between Bearsted and Hollingbourne, on the same Swanley Junction – Ashford line though on the other side of Maidstone, on a rising gradient and just past the end of a comparatively gentle curve of 150 chains radius, the locomotive's right front coupled wheel climbed the rail, travelled along the top of it for 13 feet, and then fell off on the wrong side and broke the heads of the bolts which fixed one of the fishplates, so that the end of the rail it should have run on to was bent

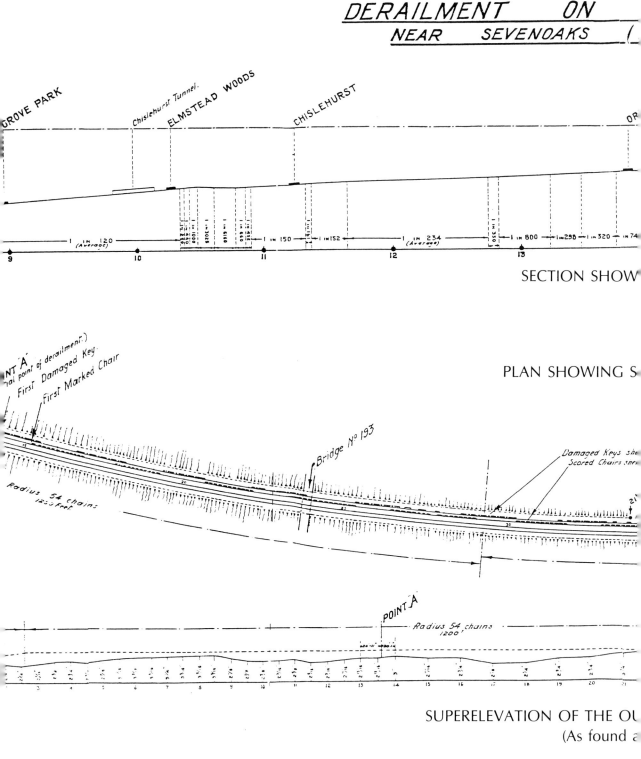

GROVE PARK

Chislehurst Tunnel.

ELMSTEAD WOODS

CHISLEHURST

OR

1 IN 120 (Average)   1 IN 150   1 IN 152   1 IN 234 (Average)   1 IN 800   1 IN 298   1 IN 320   IN 74

9   10   11   12   13

SECTION SHOW

PLAN SHOWING S

NT 'A'
(nal point of derailment.)
First Damaged Key.
First Marked Chair

Bridge Nº 193

Damaged Keys she
Scored Chairs spe

Radius 54 chains
1250 feet

POINT 'A'
Radius 54 chains
1200'

SUPERELEVATION OF THE OU
(As found a

inwards. The middle right-hand coupled wheel mounted this displaced rail and the whole engine came off the track, the train following it. The latter, three vans and eight bogie coaches, was almost wholly derailed; the engine and front van broke away from the other vehicles; several wheels became buried in the ballast. Fortunately the speed at the time was only about 40 mph, so that the shock was not what it might have been. Six passengers complained of minor injuries.

The subsequent inquiry, as on the previous occasion, brought out the unsatisfactory nature of the permanent way. As far as a point somewhere to the east of Bearsted it had recently been relayed, but then followed a 2 ½ mile stretch which had not been renewed since first being laid down when the line was built in 1883. It was due for renewal the following year, 1928. The rails themselves were in unusually good condition for their age but it was otherwise with the sleepers. Some of them had been renewed, but others still had their chairs spiked down instead of being fixed down with screws, and one in every seven of the spikes were found to be loose. The ballast was ash with a little shingle; the foundation was in clay, some of which had been working its way up through the ballast and even, in places, showed at the surface. There had been two weeks of continuous rain before the accident, and this had unsettled the foundation. In regard to drainage, a system had been installed when the first line was made, but no one now knew where the drains were; when these were excavated it was found that the drainage-holes in the cross-pipes were blocked by clay and could not take away the fallen water.

Examination of the track also revealed imperfect maintenance. At one point, where one rail should have been super-elevated, it had actually dropped by 1 ½ inches below the level of the other. The ganger in charge of the maintenance had made reports of the frequency with which attention had to be given to this stretch, but his complaints had not been taken seriously. In fact the road was simply not capable of carrying the heavier loads which were now being placed upon it. The officer who made the inspection after the derailment thought that authorisation for the use of heavy engines should not have been given, and that the lessons of the Wrotham derailment should have been learned and acted on in regard to the problem effects of a long period of bad weather. The whole track had become out of shape, the undue loading service to accentuate a deformation which was already in process through gradual subsidence. He exonerated the engine from blame. Some twelve miles of this route were then selected for immediate renewal, with due attention to be paid to the drainage, and once again six-coupled locomotives were for the time being banned from using it.

So far all the derailments had been on secondary lines and no serious casualties had been suffered. There seemed no reason why the Ks should not continue to be used on main line service, since the class had performed satisfactorily on the Central Section for a year and a half. While the original justification for building them – the turning over to them of all the best trains except the boat expresses – no longer applied, they would seem to have had a useful future on the main line from London to the Kent Coast as well as on the Redhill – Reading line, and once all the bridge-renewals on the former Chatham and Dover line had been completed they could be expected to find employment on the fast services to Chatham and the Thanet resorts. However, less than a week after the event at Bearsted something else occurred which caused the whole Class to be drastically modified. The bad weather that had contributed to the Bearsted derailment was also in part responsible for the tragedy which followed, along with insufficient permanent way maintenance and elements of chance.

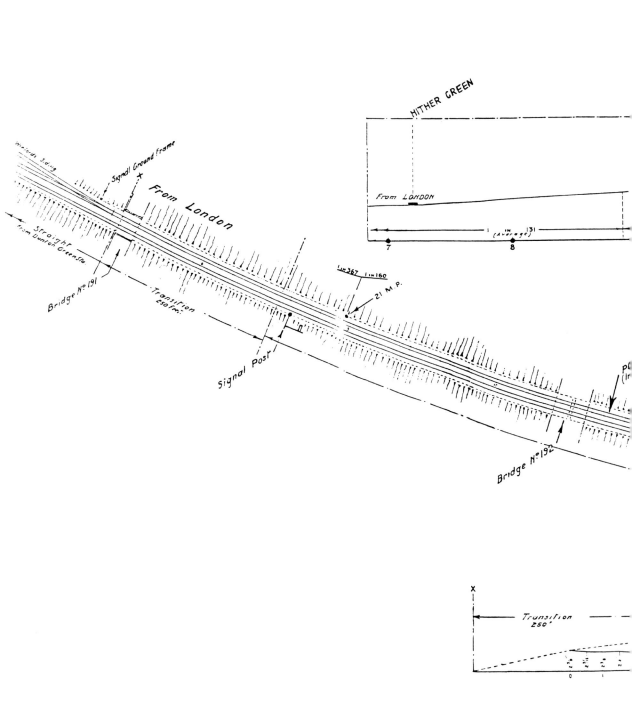

HITHER GREEN

From LONDON

7   8

Winfords Siding

Signal Ground Frame

From London

Straight
From Dunton Green Sta.

Bridge Nº 191

Transition
250 fms.

Signal Post

1 in 367 1 in 160

21 M.P.

Bridge Nº 192

X

Transition
250'

0   1

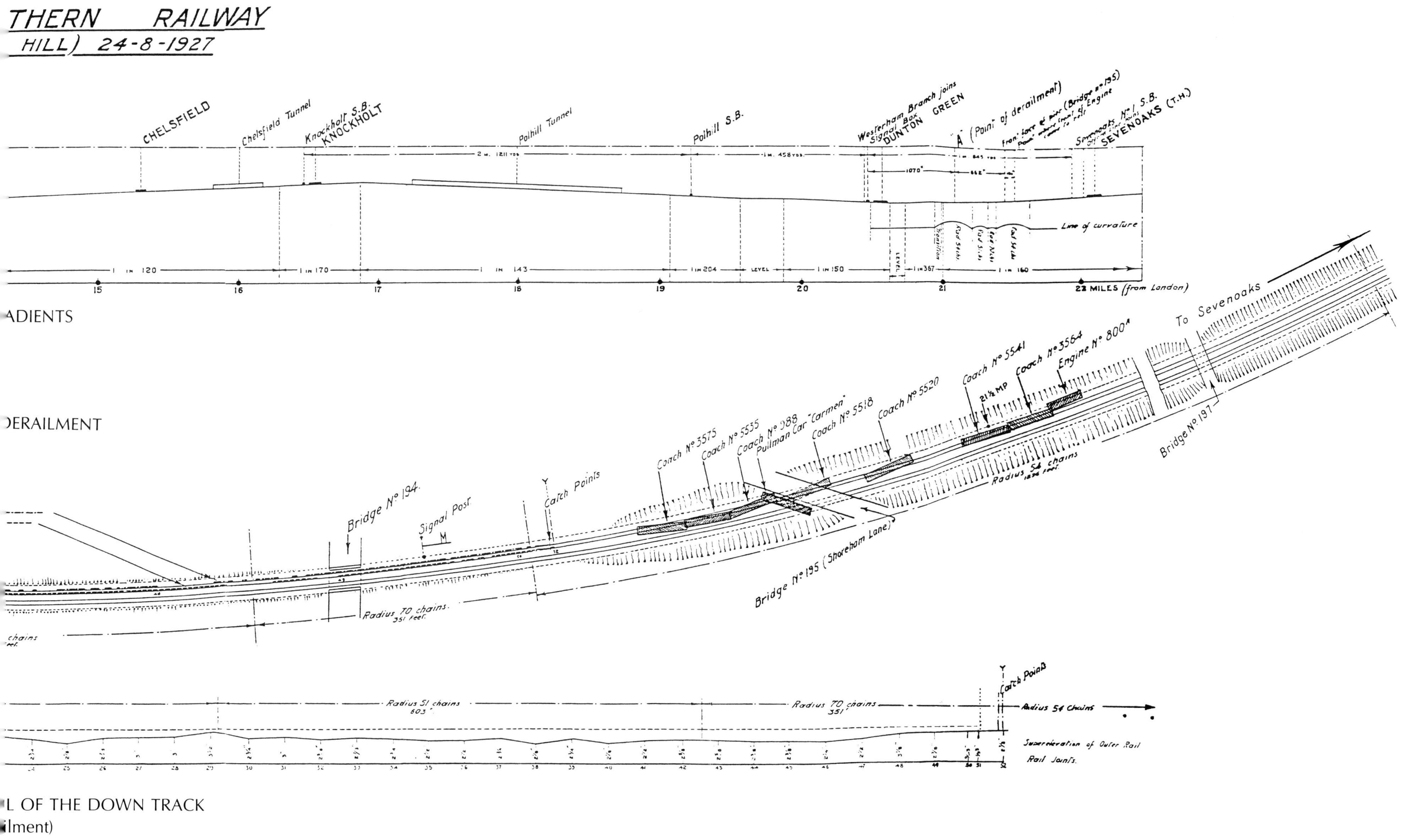

SOUTHERN RAILWAY

SEVENOAKS (BISSELL'S HILL) 24-8-1927

PLAN OF THE DOWN TRACK

Rail Joints.

Superelevation of Outer Rail

Radius 54 chains

Radius 70 chains

Radius 51 chains
603

Radius 70 chains

Radius 51 feet

Bridge No. 195 (Shoreham Lane)

Radius 54 chains
1634 feet

Bridge No. 197

Bridge No. 194

Signal Post

Catch Points

Coach No. 5518
Coach No. 5520
Coach No. 5515
Coach No. 5541
Engine No. 800A
21¾ M.P.

Pullman Car "Carmen"
Coach No. 788
Pullman Car
Coach No. 5564

DERAILMENT

To Sevenoaks

GRADIENTS

SEVENOAKS (T.H.)
Sevenoaks No. 1 S.B.
Bridge No. 195
'A' (Point of derailment)
Westerham Branch Joins
DUNTON GREEN
Polhill S.B.
Polhill Tunnel
Knockholt S.B.
Knockholt Tunnel
Chelsfield Tunnel
CHELSFIELD

23 MILES (from London)
22
21
20
19
18
17
16
15

1 in 160
1 in 367
LEVEL
1 in 150
1 in 204
LEVEL
1 in 143
1 in 170
1 in 120

Line of curvature

Catch Points

8. THE SEVENOAKS ACCIDENT

On the afternoon of Wednesday 24th August 1927 the 5 pm express for Dover and Deal backed into Cannon Street Station ready for its non-stop run to Ashford and came to rest beside one of the six wooden-planked platforms under the high arched roof which made this station a landmark for anyone going up or down the Thames – a roof which has, alas, now vanished, though the two flanking towers at the outer end still stand.

There were eight vehicles, as follows:

3rd Class corridor brake, 30 tons, built in 1924.
3 1st and 3rd corridor composites, each 32 tons, built in 1925.
First Class Pullman car *Carmen*, 30 tons, built in 1891 and reconstructed in 1920.
2 1st and 3rd corridor composites, each 32 tons, built in 1925.
1 3rd Class corridor brake, 30 tons, built in 1925.

The total tare weight of the train was therefore 250 tons.

All the coaches were of recent build with the exception of the Pullman car and had steel panelling and under-frames. The Pullman, a massive vehicle, as heavy as the others though 8 feet shorter, had been given a steel underframe when rebuilt, but still had wooden sides; when choosing to travel in it one paid for luxury rather than safety, though probably no one entering it and regarding its opulent interior would have had such thoughts. It was one of a batch built by the Gilbert Car Manufacturing Company of Troy, New York, shipped to this country in sections and assembled at Ashford; it was mounted on standard SER bogies and seated on-ly 24 passengers. All the coaches were lit by electricity generated in under-coach dynamos worked from the bogie axles; the Pullman in addition had gas cylinders which supplied a small oven used for preparing light meals and refreshments. The train contained more than the usual proportion of first Class accommodation; like the corresponding morning up train it was a prestige service.

The engine provided to haul it was No. A 800, *River Cray*, the first of the Brighton-built batch of Ks which, as mentioned in the previous chapter, had come off the rails in a siding at Maidstone earlier in the month but had apparently suffered no damage. Driver F.H. Buss was a senior man who had been in the Company's ser-vice, first on the SER, then on the SECR, then on the SR, for forty years, and had been driving for thirty. His usual engine was an L 4-4-0, but he had some familiari-ty with the Ks. His fireman, H.C Barrer, had never fired on a K before and told Buss so when he joined him. The guard, W Bailey, travelled in the rear coach. The train was fairly full, as would be expected on a return business service, with many of the passengers using season tickets. Among them were a locomotive inspector coming off duty, a locomotive driver returning to his shed 'on the cushions', one or two titled persons, and at least one medical doctor; there were also a number of children travelling with their parents. Just as the train was about to leave some late arrivals ran up to the barrier hoping to be able to board the train, but the ticket collector at the barrier refused them admittance to the platform, to their immediate annoyance – but no doubt they felt grateful to him afterwards.

It had been a day of heavy rain in the South East of England; indeed the whole month had been unwonted-ly wet. In Kent itself it dried up after twelve o'clock, but in the City another heavy shower was falling as the train pulled out of the terminus about half a minute after its advertised time. As it threaded the curves to London Bridge and then gathered speed on the level length to New Cross it may have lost a little more time because of the wet rail; however, it was not usual with this train to hurry over the initial exit from London in case one trod on the tail of an electric train in front. On this par-ticular service it was quite customary to lose one or two minutes as far as Sevenoaks and to recover them later by fast running downhill to Tonbridge and along the gently rising stretch which followed.

No adverse signals were sighted until the approach to Orpington, when, on somewhat easier grades then the earlier 1 in 120 to Elmstead Woods, 40 mph had been attained. Buss blew his whistle, and the signal arm fell at once, so the check here was only slight. Knockholt summit, at the top of the following rise, which brought the speed down to about 35 mph, was passed a few minutes later; a little way beyond was the entrance to Polhill tunnel, where the line passes under the main ridge of the North Downs.

Buss knew from experience that a 'River' was apt to roll somewhat on the open downhill stretch beyond the tunnel, and took steps to moderate the speed. To quote from the record of the Ministry of Transport Enquiry:

"'After passing Knockholt up distant signal, where the gradient begins to fall (650 yards from the North end of Polhill tunnel) he told his fireman to shut the front and open the back damper, because they had 200 lb of steam and a full boiler of water. He thought that this would check any tendency of the engine to roll on emerging from the tunnel. This was the first occasion the fireman had been with him, and he was not certain whether he would be aware of the possibility of the engine rolling after it had passed through the tunnel. He desired therefore to keep the speed of the train within limits. Although he knew he had lost half a minute at Polhill tunnel he had no intention or wish to make up time – to do this would have been to run the engine at a higher speed than he thought desirable.'

It is necessary to emphasize this because much of what had been written about this accident, then and after-wards, owes more to imagination than to evidence. In

The wreckage of the 5 pm from Cannon Street just north of the Shoreham Lane bridge abutment on 24th August 1927. The Pullman coach 'Carmen' struck the stonework sideways-on and fell apart into sections; the coach immediately ahead of it was crushed between it and the bridge and was completely smashed up; most of the fatalities occurred in that vehicle.
Courtesy: Locomotive Club of Great Britain Ken Nunn Collection

his otherwise excellent book *Red for Danger* L.T.C Rolt speaks of the train going through Polhill Tunnel at six-ty miles an hour and rocking violently as it did so. No such speed could possibly have been reached inside the tunnel; according to evidence adduced at the inquiry the train had barely reached this speed at Dunton Green at the bottom of the dip before Sevenoaks, nor did anyone allege that the train had been riding unsteadily up to that point.

According to Buss, Dunton Green was passed at from 55 to 57 miles an hour. Then came the first sign that something was wrong - a loud knocking noise from the front of the engine, which was audible in the front coach of the train. Buss, who was in any case about to shut off steam before negotiating the curve through Sevenoaks, did so at once, but the knocking continued so he ap-plied the train's brakes, which did not seem to operate as quickly as they should. Over the next quarter of a minute events built up to the final catastrophe. What had happened when the noise was heard was that the engine had left the rails and was riding over the sleeper chairs. It then burst a set of catch points, so that the whole train became derailed.

At Shoreham Lane Bridge the down line went beneath a single arch, with an abutment to the left and a supporting pier to the right. The locomotive, leaning to one side, struck violently against the abutment on its left; the front buffer beam was pushed right back; the left-hand cylinder was smashed; the piston rod, piston valve rod and all the motion except the connecting and coupling rods were buckled up; both the footstep plates were ripped off. The left-hand tank and the left side of the cab were damaged, and some damage was also done to the right-hand top side of the cab through its strik-ing the pier of the bridge. A little further on the left-hand front Bissel truck wheel came off its axle and was found with three spokes broken. The locomotive finally came to rest a little over 100 yards beyond the bridge, tilted against the side of the cutting, with the remains of the Bissel truck crumpled up beneath the front driving axle.

The whole train became derailed as it was dragged along, and the couplings of some of the coaches snap-ped. The two vehicles immediately behind the engine remained attached to it and suffered severely from the battering they received as they were scraped along the bridge abutment. The two vehicles behind broke away, and the second one fared worse than any of the others; it first slewed right across the track and was then push-ed by the heavy Pullman car behind it so that it was com-pletely smashed to pieces against the abutment. Most of the fatalities occurred in this vehicle. The Pullman car also landed up sideways between the abutment and the pier, and the coach which followed it crashed into it at the right-hand rear end; here too there were fatal casualties, but mercifully the lighted gas burners did not start a fire. Only the last two coaches escaped serious damage.

Twelve passengers were killed outright and one died later in hospital. Twenty were seriously injured, including the fireman who suffered a broken arm. Forty more were less seriously hurt or suffered from shock. A further seventy-one later made written complaints to the railway company alleging they had been injured or shocked. Including all the latter, that made a total of 144 casualties, which was probably more than half of those who were travelling.

Help arrived promptly from many quarters; uninjured passengers did what they could to extricate and help the injured, and ambulances were soon on the scene to convey the latter to neighbouring hospitals. The dead were taken to the waiting room at Sevenoaks station to await identification. In one case, a 33-year-old woman who lived at Elham, near Folkestone, the only way of establishing identity was through the clothing and jewellery she wore.

It was the Southern Railway's first serious accident, and the first for some years to have occurred in the vicinity of London. It also happened during August, when the press had less to engage its attention than usual and were not unwilling to 'go to town' on the accident. At that time a well-known song, made popular by the singer Paul Robeson, was 'Ol' Man river', who 'just kept rolling'. Not surprisingly the fact that the locomotive involved was one of the 'River' type led to the whole Class being termed the 'Rolling Rivers', and there was a tendency to lay the whole blame on its design. Local papers in general confined themselves to straight reporting and to recording the remarks and reactions of passengers and bystanders. Among the more bizarre happenings mentioned by survivors was the experience of losing their laced-up shoes and then finding them afterwards in the wreckage, though their feet had suffered no injuries. There was also the usual tales of miraculous escapes through last-minute decisions not to take that train.

The disaster had two immediate consequences. One was the recall of Maunsell from Italy, where he was on holiday, to give evidence about the locomotive to the Ministry of Transport Inspector at the enquiry which was to be held. The other was an order that, pending the results of this investigation, all K Class tank engines were to be confiend to their sheds.

9. EVIDENCE AT THE INQUIRY

On 16th January 1928 Colonel Sir John Pringle, CB, who had been appointed by the Minister of Transport to conduct the Inquiry into the Sevenoaks accident, finished and signed his lengthy report. It had been a long business, of which the shortest part had been the taking of statements and hearing evidence; after that had come the carrying out of investigations and the making of tests both in regard to the locomotive that had been derailed and to the track over which the derailment had occurred, which he thought necessary in order to reach a true opinion about an accident which, whatever what some clamorous voices might say, did not seem to have any single obvious cause. The Report, when completed, reflected a fair and balanced judgement and is worth reading for its own sake, being lucid, well-written and straight forward without jargon or incomprehensibilities.

When a railway accident occurs there is seldom a simple answer to the question: Why did it happen? what went wrong? Behind the immediate cause there will be many contributory causes that do not become apparent until an Inquiry has been held and evidence taken and considered. Sheer chance may play a part; so may the carelessness or shoddy work of someone long beforehand, as in the Tay Bridge disaster of 1879, when malpractice on the part of the builders together with insufficient foresight on the part of the designer led to the high girders collapsing in a furious gale just as a train was passing over them. Here was an example of an accident waiting to happen. To some extent the Sevenoaks accident was one of this kind. A great many conducive factors operating together, some from the present and some from the past, brought it about; the locomotive's propensity to roll in certain circumstances was by no means the most important factor.

The Report begins with a brief summary of the events of the half-hour which elapsed after the train had left Cannon Street. Then follows a description of the site of the accident, given in some detail, with drawings added to elucidate it. Next come details about the engine, No. A 800, *River Cray* - its dimensions, characteristics and special features. After that follow the statements, in reported speech, of various witnesses of the event and of people who had been responsible for designing the locomotive and maintaining the track. A number of drivers who had knowledge of the K type were also asked for their opinions. At the end Sir John set out the relevant points that had arisen, referred to the investigations which he had asked should be made, advanced his own conclusions based on what he had seen and heard, and added certain recommendations for the Company's attention.

The evidence given at the inquiry consisted of the following:

1. Statements by signalmen at Knockholt, Polhill, Dunton Green and Sevenoaks No. 1 signal boxes as to the passing of the derailed train.
2. Statements by the driver, fireman and guard of the derailed train.
3. Accounts of the experience of a number of persons who had travelled as passengers in the train.
4. Statements made by the driver and fireman of the preceding down train.
5. Statements made by the other drivers who had also driven K Class locomotives.
6. Statements from the Locomotive Running Superintendent and from the locomotive foremen at Bricklayers Arms and Dover locomotive depots.
7. A statement by R.E.L. Maunsell, Chief Mechanical Engineer.
8. Statements from G Ellson, Chief Engineer, and members of his staff.
9. Special evidence given by driver A.W. Payne, a senior and very experienced man who was familiar with the K Class engines and had driven most of them, and who had been present at the trials carried out on the LNER and SR (Western Section) main lines (to be referred to in the next chapter).

From all these disclosures one may select certain parts as specially significant.

The signalmen from the four signal-boxes stated what the approximate time had been when the train had passed them (except in the case of Sevenoaks No. 1 box, which was never reached), what the weather was like at the time and what in their judgement was the approximate speed of the train when it passed their box. In general, as they estimated the latter, it was the usual speed at which it passed, and agreed in regard to Dunton Green with the estimates of the driver and fireman; certainly it was not excessive. It is interesting to note the smart efficiency of the man on duty in the Sevenoaks box, who at 5.30 pm heard two bangs and saw that both up and down roads were shown on his instruments as 'Occupied'. Realising this meant that there had been an accident which had caused both lines to be fouled, he at once sent an 'Obstruction Danger' call to both Dunton Green and Sevenoaks No. 2 boxes, on either side of his, thus preventing the possibility of another train running into the derailed vehicles.

Driver Buss, fireman Barter and guard Bailey described the events as they had experienced them. The former's account, as written in the Report, was as follows:

"The engine ran steadily without any unusual movement through Polhill Tunnel to Dunton Green station, where Buss estimated that the speed attained was from 55 to 57 miles an hour. About half way between Dunton Green and Sevenoaks, when steam was still applied, the engine running as usual, he heard a knocking noise in front of the engine and immediately closed the regulator. After the usual clattering noise, due to shutting off steam, had ceased, the knocking noise began again, and then he applied the brake with full effect. He thought he made this application just where the catch points are situated on the down line. He had not felt any extraordinary movement or lift of the engine wheels before he first heard the knocking noise mentioned. He thought this noise was made by the Bissel front wheels being off the rails to the left, and held strongly the opinion that it could not have been the leading coupled wheels of the engine. He did not feel that the continuous brake was getting a hold upon the wheels until the engine was near the Shoreham Lane overbridge. Buss drove from the right-hand side of the footplate, and remembered that the right-hand top side of the cab scraped the pier of the bridge as they passed through it. He never made any complaints to the Locomotive Branch on account of the rough riding or rolling of these tank engines. He thought them good for their work, but liable to roll if they attained a speed of more that 50 miles per hour. Rolling was set up sometimes on these engines when passing over crossings, and did not always die away for some little time, though less than a minute. He thought the rolling motion was greater than on a tender engine, possibly owing to the movement of water from side to side in the tanks. When he experienced considerable rolling he had endeavoured to steady the engine by closing the regulator and thereby reducing speed.

Fireman Barter's evidence was consistent with that of Buss, and added a little to it:

"He had never ridden on the footplate of a 'River' Class tank engine, and told Driver Buss so before getting on engine No. 800. He had heard in conversation with drivers that tank engines of this class were powerful and efficient; also that the fireman's work, from the point of view of working the injectors and keeping a nice fire going, was easier than on other engines. He had also heard that these engines rolled somewhat at high speed, but not to a dangerous extent; the movement differed in this respect from the usual swaying movement on tender engines. About half way through Polhill tunnel driver Buss told him to reverse the dampers, which he did. He was also told to put a little coal on the fire, so that it should not be necessary to do any firing whilst travelling down the bank, in order that the risk of being thrown about on the footplate should be avoided. He did not however, think there was more movement on the engine after emerging from Polhill tunnel than that to which he was accustomed on other engines. He had no idea that anything went wrong until they were within 100 – 150 yards of the catch points. He then heard the noise of a crack in front of the engine as if something had broken. His driver, on hearing this sound, closed the regulator and practically at the same time applied the continuous brake – at first partially and then fully. Some time had elapsed since he had worked other than goods and mixed traffic trains, and he was unable to compare the speed on this occasion with that on other occasions when he had travelled down the bank, or to give any information as to the speed at which the train was travelling at any point of the journey. They had a full head of steam, a full boiler of water and a big fire burning at the time of the derailment".

Guard Bailey, who had several times officiated on this train, stated that he had tested the vacuum brake's efficiency from his van at the rear of the train; the gauge reading had been 21 inches. They had left Cannon Street a little late and had passed Knockholt at 24½ minutes past 5, and Dunton Green 4½ minutes later; his estimate of the train's speed at that point was between 55 and 60 mph, 'not running noticeably faster than usual'. He had noticed nothing unusual in the movement of the train until the continuous brake was applied.

Seven other persons in the train described the event as each of them had experienced it, in all the vehicles except the third and fourth. Two, being servants of the Company, were the most professionally observant. Locomotive Inspector Turner had been in the last compartment of the front coach or the first of the second coach – he could not be sure which – and was a frequent traveller on this train, which did not usually reach its maximum speed until a point between Tonbridge and Ashford. On this occasion they were doing about 56 at Dunton Green. Half way between the latter station and Sevenoaks 'the carriage began to bump, not because it was off the rails, but throwing from one side to side and knocking against the rails.' It was not serious enough to indicate danger. The knocking died out, but within a few seconds there was a smash and the vehicle became derailed. The brake was not applied at the moment he experienced this severe jolting. He had ridden on the footplate of a 'River' on one occasion when it had been reported for rolling badly, and had observed this to happen near Cheriton Junction; he had reported at the time that the condition of the road had something to do with the rolling.

Driver Perry was riding as a passenger in the second compartment of the first carriage. He had occasionally driven engines of the 'River' Class. Half way between Dunton Green and Sevenoaks he had heard a click which seemed to come from the engine; it was a noise, not a movement, and he had thought it was due to the driver closing the regulator. After hearing the noise he experienced nothing unusual in the carriage's movement until the engine and coach became derailed.

Conductor Mansell, from the Pullman car *Carmen*, also declared that this was the first time in his period of service on this train, two years in all, that he had noticed anything unusual in the riding of the vehicle. On this occasion there had been an unusual rolling after passing Dunton Green, then a steadying-down, then the derailment happening very suddenly.

These testimonies, along with those of the other passengers questioned, generally agreed in showing that, as far as the train was concerned, there was one point where there had been an unusual movement, but that subsequent to it nothing else untoward appeared to happen until the moment of derailment.

The driver and fireman of the preceding train, the 4.30 pm from Charing Cross to Sevenoaks, which stopped at all stations and was hauled by a Wainwright C Class 0-6-0 described its progress between Orpington and Sevenoaks. There had been no unusual movement of the engine, nor any undue oscillation, at any time. Sir John's object in calling for their evidence was to ascertain whether the track itself had been safe at slow speeds a few minutes before the passing of the express. It obviously had, but the rate of travel of this preceding train had been very moderate - not more than 40 mph before Dunton Green and as little as 15 over the part of the track where the accident had happened.

Two drivers, W. Gooding and F. Donaldson, contributed their experiences of riding on the footplate of a 'River' Class engine. Gooding mentioned a tendency to roll at certain places, one being the accident site and another the straight stretch between Tonbridge and Paddock Wood at Tudely. His practice when this happened was to apply the train brake and steady the engine. Donaldson generally agreed with him, and suggested that the fault might not altogether be in the engine, and that the condition of the track in certain places had something to do with it. It is at this point that the state of permanent way begins to come into the picture as a contributory cause.

The Locomotive Running Superintendent, A.D. Jones, and the locomotive foremen at Bricklayers Arms and Dover depots were next questioned. Jones explained how complaints about the running of locomotives were passed on to him in writing, and referred to the 'Rivers' in particular. He mentioned the prototype which (as explained above) had for a long while worked the down early morning newspaper train from Cannon Street to Ashford and come back on the 8.10 am Folkestone Junction to Cannon Street, about which no complaints in regard to rolling had ever been received until 1925. Only one complaint had ever been lodged against this engine, two weeks prior to the accident, which was not so much about the way it was behaving as about the state of the track where the unsteadiness showed itself, on a straight section. He also mentioned the derailment in the sidings at Maidstone, which of course had nothing to do with any tendency to roll. He reckoned that the 'Rivers' were quite suitable for a road that was in thorough order and capable of taking any class of engine which had been accepted for running over it, with superelevation kept as it should be, and with no weak rail-joints. It was the Chief Engineer who gave permission for the use of a particular type of locomotive on a stated section, after receiving a diagram of which it contained the details that would enable him to make a judgement.

The two foremen, G.W. Oxley and E.N. Corner, reported what complaints had been received by them; they had been few. Oxley added that drivers spoke quite freely to him, and he would have heard of it if they had thought the Ks were unfit and unsafe for traffic. Corner gave it as the general opinion of those drivers he had talked to, that while the 'Rivers' rolled more than tender engines did, they never did this to a dangerous extent.

The next witness was Maunsell himself. He first gave a lengthy account of the preliminary planning and building of the prototype, its testing, the ordering and delayed construction of the subsequent two production batches and their use both on the Central and Eastern Sections since that time. He asserted that no complaints had been received in regard to any of the first production batch, Nos. 791 – 799, during the 1½ years while they were being used on the Brighton line. The second batch, Nos 800 – 809, included improvements which had already been made to the prototype, and it was about some of *these* ten locomotives that complaints of rolling had been received while they were operating on the Eastern Section. In each instance the engine had been taken out of service and sent either to Ashford or to Brighton for examination and, if necessary, for repair.

He then referred to the three derailments of 'Rivers' on the Swanley to Ashford line, in consequence of which this type had for the time being banned from using it, along with the heavier engines of the 'King Arthur' and 'Lord Nelson' tender classes. He further disclosed that since the Sevenoaks accident all the 'Rivers' had been taken out of service pending further inquiry on the instruction of the General Manager.

He then went on to mention experiments made since the derailment at Ashford, to see whether it was likely to have been the leading wheels of the front truck or the coupled wheels which had first left the track. Deliberate attempts to force the former off the rail had succeeded, but it was then found that they fell too low and went too wide off the rail to have made the marks on the keys and chairs which were actually found after the derailment. It therefore seemed that these marks must have been due to the first pair of coupled wheels coming off the rails. He had not at first thought that was possible, but had been obliged to change his mind. Although deliberate attempts to force these wheels off the rails had been unsuccessful while the engine was stationary, it was not impossible that this could happen if it were travelling at high speed. In fact such a thing had happened before on the LBSCR in 1914, when two recently built 4-6-4 tank locomotives had derailed while at the head of a train in motion - in one case at high speed. He thought that on a good track a tank engine was no more liable to oscillate than a tender engine, but that a different nature of oscillation occurred. With tank locomotives the period of oscillation was, he thought, longer, due to the moment of inertia of the tanks, and therefore more dangerous.

With the next group of witnesses the interest moved from the locomotive to the track it was using. G. Ellson, the Southern Railway's Chief Engineer, provided some plans and sections of the part of the line where the derailment occurred, together with a survey of the gauge and superelevation of the rails on the down line, measurements of the latter being noted for every half-length of rail. He indicated where the marks on the rails showed just where the derailment had occurred. The first

.... was a score, 23 feet 1 inch in length, commencing at the inside of a left-hand rail, across the head of the rail, to the outside, showing the travel of a flange of a left-hand engine wheel. The damage to the down road, up to the point of complete derailment, was caused in his view by the swaying of engine No. 800 with one pair of wheels derailed on the left-hand side of the track i.e. the inside of the curve .... He did not think that there had been any material increase in the speed of trains during the last seven years, but that the weight of the trains had been considerably increased. He thought that the lack of superelevation of 1 inch on a curve of 54 chains' radius certainly called for attention. But he did not think that a difference of level of this extent, unless it occurred at regular intervals and over a long distance, would set up such rolling or oscillation as it would cause anything more than serious discomfort.

His subordinate, C.A.G. Linton, the Divisional Engineer in charge of the permanent way between London and Tonbridge, said that the track was renewed every 2½ years except in Polhill tunnel, where owing to atmospheric conditions, it was done every five years. He had no reports of difficulties in keeping the rails to gauge, line and elevation; however, the damage done to the track when the accident occurred had made a relaying necessary. He had personally inspected the track and the bank on that particular curve just a week beforehand, and had been quite satisfied with their condition then.

Six of his subordinates, including the ganger and subganger who regularly walked this section of track, and whose duty it was to keep in order, also gave evidence.

Several important points emerged from what they said:

1. Wet weather sometimes caused the road to subside very quickly.
2. To all appearances the road had been in good order late in the afternoon when the accident happened.
3. The bottom ballast was assumed to be in good order but had not been examined.
4. The level of the cess on the inside of the curve may have been too high to allow for efficient drainage.
5. Gangers were informed of the cant needed on particular curves by a card from the Chief Engineers's office; in the case of this particular curve the superelevation should be 3¼ inches.
6. The oscillation on the engine which caused it to derail probably began when it passed over a trailing siding connection near Dunton Green station.

This concluded the evidence taken by Sir John Pringle before the investigations and tests were made which are described in the next chapter. Sir John also thought it advisable to make his own personal examination of the damaged engine, and to arrange to have some tests run on a stretch of well-maintained track with a sister engine to see whether in those circumstances it exhibited any tendency to roll, before he finally made up his mind about the causes of the disaster.

Front Cover: No. A 793 'River Ouse' heading the southbound 'Southern Belle' Pullman from Victoria to Brighton during 1925. These engines coped with this sometimes heavy train as well as the somewhat older 'Baltic' tanks, which L. Billinton had built during 1914 – 1922 for this duty, although they were not as large. They were not much liked by the Central Section crews, however, since they were unsteady at speed over imperfectly-maintained track. *Courtesy: Lens of Sutton*

Back Cover: After being de-railed at the head of the 5 pm from Cannon Street to Dover and Deal on 24th August 1927, No. A 800 'River Cray' lies on its side against the wall of the cutting beyond the Shoreham Lane Bridge. Note that the front Bissel truck with the leading wheels is no longer attached to the frame but lies crushed beneath it, the wheels having been knocked off. The leading coach is badly damaged; that behind it, though de-railed, is in a better state. *Courtesy: Kent County Library*

10. INVESTIGATIONS DURING THE INQUIRY

Sir John Pringle was nothing if not thorough. He had gained a wide experience of railways and their working during his career as an Army officer and had been involved in their wartime organisation in this country. In regard to the Sevenoaks accident, he did not confine the inquest merely to taking statements and considering them, but looked for more direct evidence to enable him to come to a decision. He therefore asked the railway authorities to make a thorough inspection of the part of the line where the engine had been derailed (the results of which are mentioned in the previous chapter) and himself went to Ashford, where the damaged engine had been towed, to inspect it for himself. He knew that he was dealing with a type rather than a single machine, and therefore requested that tests should be made, both of a sister-engine to the damaged one and of the three-cylinder example, No. A 890, on a piece of track which could not be faulted, since if the trouble lay with the locomotive rather than the permanent way it could be expected to manifest itself even on perfect track.

In regard to the inspection of the permanent way between Dunton Green and the accident site, the markings on the tops of the rails and at their sides over the keys and the chairs showed that the locomotive was certainly rolling, and that the side-to-side movement, when the engine had left the rails, was very considerable, so that it was possible to estimate the amplitude of the roll; and this had gradually increased up to the fifth full movement from left to right and had then decreased noticeably just before a set of catch points was reached; here the left-hand wheels of the locomotive had burst the stock rail so that the whole train became derailed as it passed over them. It was possible to measure the distances when the main weight of the engine pressed first on the outside keys of the left-hand rail and then on the inside chairs of the right-hand rail; and these distances, Pringles observed,

"..... are interesting, I think, as showing the liability, at all events of a tank engine of this Class, to increase a roll which has been set up, especially when on a curve where there is irregularity in the superelevation. It will be agreed that, as a rule, the longer the roll, to the greater extent will the wheels lift and the danger increase".

No. A 800 had been towed to Ashford on its coupled and rear bogie wheels, the remains of the Bissel truck having been removed. Pringle went to look at the engine and concluded that the damage to the track could not have been due to the truck which supported the front, since when the wheels of a similar truck on a sister engine were deliberately forced off the rails by pressure applied sideways they hung down much further than

the 1½ inches which the wheels that had done the damage to the permanent way had actually descended, so that more damage than had been observed would have been evident. It seemed clear to him that the wheel which had first left the rail must have been the left-hand one on the front coupled axle. Such a thing was known to have occurred before with the 4-6-4 LBSCR tank engine at Hassocks in 1914. The slides of the Bissel truck showed little signs of being scratched. The axle boxes of the coupled wheels also appeared to have moved freely in their horn guides.

"The results of this examination, and of the trials at Ashford, were sufficient in my opinion to prove that the Bissel axle was not that first derailed, that the left-hand Bissel wheel was forced off its axle as the result of its coming into violent contact with some obstruction after the engine was completely derailed, whereby spokes in the wheel were broken and the bore in the hole of the wheel-boss distorted. Further, that with regard to the markings found on the engine wheels, and the out-of-truth in the frame, connecting rods, etc., these were such as were likely to have resulted either from the derailment of one of the coupled engine axles, or from subsequent complete derailment. My inspection of engine No. 800, therefore, in its damaged condition justified the conclusion that no such radical defect in design or condition existed as would in itself have caused the derailment. Also, that the axle first derailed was the leading coupled axle. In this there is, it appears, complete concurrence by both Civil and Mechanical Engineers of the Company".

Sir John also made a personal examination of the permanent way onwards from the point where derailment first occurred. The rails, old though they were and due for renewal the following year, seemed to him satisfactory as to strength and condition, and the chairs and sleepers also appeared satisfactory. However, he was critical of the quality of the ballast. The upper part of the latter was a mixture of broken fragments of Kentish ragstone and a binding material; further down, beneath the sleepers, immediately under each rail and for 18 inches on either side of it, there was a mixture of ragstone and beach ballast; all the rest was beach ballast with binding material. He thought the quality of the ballast, and of the bottom ballast in particular, was inferior in rigidity and holding capacity to the sort which was found to be on first class roads elsewhere. It appeared, too, that in places the bottom ballast had sunk into the formation, and that the track had consequently subsided, so that there could be no drainage except through the bank at the side.

He observed also that the permanent way staff had failed to keep the superelevation of the right hand rail at the level prescribed in the Chief Engineer's published table, and that the irregularities were considerable, to the extent that they were likely to induce rolling on any type of engine. They were also a number of irregularities in gauge. Heavy loads moved at high speed had damaged the foundation of the permanent way over a number of years, and the excessive rainfall of the previous few weeks had impaired it still more. He thought that the permanent way staff either did not realise how much the road had suffered under the combined effects of heavy traffic and wet weather, or were unable to maintain it.

Sir John also felt he needed fuller information about how much the 'River' tanks oscillated at high speed in comparison with a tender locomotive of similar weight and power. To ascertain this it was necessary to find a section of main line railway track that was in good order, over which high speeds were regularly run by heavy locomotives, and which included a certain amount of curvature. The London & North Eastern Railway authorities agreed to allow two miles of their main line route from King's Cross to the North to be used, between mile-posts 54¼ and 56¼ just south of Offord station; these included the well-known curves along the banks of the River Ouse (now to some extent straightened out). Mr H.N. Gresley, the LNER's Chief Mechanical Engineer, agreed to associate himself with Pringle in the tests to be carried out and to report upon them. 'River' Class tank engines Nos. 803 (2-cylinder) and 890 (3-cylinder) were taken there, together with 'King Arthur' 4-6-0 No. E 782, *Sir Brian*, and on 16th October the trials were made, A.W. Payne, one of the SR's most senior drivers, who had a long experience of 'Rivers', operating the locomotives in turn. Gresley provided a portable accelerometer for recording vertical and lateral accelerations on the footplate, and two vehicles to be hauled, one of which was the LNER dynamometer car.

The subsequent report furnished by Gresley showed that both the tank engines tested ran smoothly with only the slightest degree of rolling, No. 890 being rather the livelier of the two on its springs. The interesting thing about these trials was the fact that the 'King Arthur', while running without either rolling or lurching, vibrated so much that no record could be obtained by the accelerometer. The runs were made both with full and with nearly empty side tanks, and at speeds which varied between the upper fifties and the lower eighties. So far, so good. Gresley was favourably impressed by both tank engines.

However, the SR's General Manager, Sir Herbert Walker, asked for a similar series of tests to be carried out on SR metals, and a seven-mile stretch between Woking and Walton-on-Thames was chosen, rather straighter than the LNER section used for the previous trials, though having one reverse curve. The whole section was given prior attention by the permanent way staff, when a number of faults were corrected, before the trials began on 30th October. A somewhat different picture then emerged. In eight down and eight up runs, half with full and half with nearly empty tanks, there was

much more rolling on the part of the 'Rivers', though never to the point of appearing dangerous. The speeds attempted were not on the whole as high as on the LNER. Again the 'King Arthur' vibrated badly, even more than before, and also rolled in places, which it had not previously done. It was, in Gresley's words, 'very rough and uncomfortable'. The latter's general conclusions included the following remarks:

"There is little difference between the running of the two tank engines. Compared with the tender engine they ride more softly and more comfortably. When on a bad piece of road the period of the roll of the tank engines is longer and easier but, I think, of greater amplitude. The tender engine has stiffer springs, and consequently rides more rigidly and the roll is shorter. I should expect the running of the tender engine would be more detrimental to the road at high speeds than that of the tank engines. The two-cylinder engine No. 803 is slightly steadier than the three-cylinder No.890, probably because No. 803 has laminated springs on the pony truck and bogie, whereas on No. 890 helical springs are used .... I think engine 890 would probably ride as well as 803 if laminated springs were fitted to the pony truck and bogie. In other respects 890 is the better engine of the two. When running backwards, bunker first, with the bogies leading, the riding of both tank engines was distinctly steadier than running forwards with the pony truck leading. Both engines ran noticeably steadier when water tanks and coal bunkers were full than when they were practically empty ..... Both the tank and tender engines ran with remarkable steadiness at high speeds on the London and North Eastern track. The curves are all transition curves, and the general condition of the road was superior to that of the Southern. I am satisfied that on the London and North Eastern section of the road over which the trials were made both tank and tender engines could run regularly with safety at any speed which they could attain.

On the trial section of the Southern Railway the rolling of both tank and tender engines was excessive at high speeds; the rolling of the engines at some places when running on the straight line was quite as great as the worst roll experienced on curves. It seemed clear to me that this rolling was caused by irregular depression of the road at various points, apparently owing to the sleepers not being properly packed, and to defective drainage.

The rolling of both tank and tender engines at speeds of 70 miles and hour is greater than I consider to be safe for regular working on roads in a condition similar to that of the Southern Railway over which the trials were made. If the location of the irregular depressions in the road previously referred to should coincide with the rolling periods of engines, a dangerous and unstable condition would arise. As it is not so likely that such irregularities would occur as close to each other as to coincide with the shorter rolling periods of tender engines, there is less possibility of this dangerous condition arising with tender engines than with tank engines. Both the tank engines are well-designed efficient engines, and on a road well laid and well maintained are suitable for working express passenger trains".

J.L.M. Moore, an official in the Ministry of Transport who also rode on the engines on both sets of tests, and made his own separate report, generally agreed with Gresley. The upshot of the trials may be summarised as follows:

1. Both tank engine types were perfectly satisfactory on well-maintained track at high speeds; whatever rolling occurred was too slight to worry about.

2. On imperfectly-maintained track (a condition which of course should never be found where high speed running is expected) weak spots on the road produced rolling movements, whether or not the line was curved.

3. When the tank engines travelled with the bogies, not the pony trucks, leading, the riding was a little smoother.

4. The hard springing in the tender engine was likely to damage the permanent way.

So the verdict reached at the end of these trials, so far as the K Class tank engines were concerned, would seem to have been 'Not Guilty'. Perhaps they should have been acquitted - but, as will be seen, that was not what actually happened.

NAMES OF 'RIVER' CLASS TANKS

790	RIVER AVON		800	RIVER CRAY
791	RIVER ADUR		801	RIVER DARENTH
792	RIVER ARUN		802	RIVER CUCKMERE
793	RIVER OUSE		803	RIVER ITCHEN
794	RIVER ROTHER		804	RIVER TAMAR
795	RIVER MEDWAY		805	RIVER CAMEL
796	RIVER STOUR		806	RIVER TORRIDGE
797	RIVER MOLE		807	RIVER AXE
798	RIVER WEY		808	RIVER CHAR
799	RIVER TEST		809	RIVER DART

11. VERDICT AND CONSEQUENCES

On the strength of the information he had gained from evidence given verbally, the locomotive trials mentioned above and some statistics which he had requested[1], Sir John Pringle came to his conclusions about the causes of the Sevenoaks accident.

He observed that it was one, like so many others, in which clear proofs as to failure of mechanism, serious faults in the track, or the existence of some obstruction were lacking; he nonetheless thought that some relevant facts had emerged. The passage of a train stopping at all stations over the portion of track where the accident had occurred at least showed that the permanent way had been in a good enough state for the movement of a train at low speed. The 5 pm from Cannon Street, on the other hand, had been travelling at a much higher speed which, he estimated, could not well have been less than 60 mph and might have been more[2]. Unusual movements had been reported – rolling, oscillation, violent jolting and lurching – in both engine and train during the period when the former had been partially derailed. The type of tank engine in question was, by general agreement of all the drivers he had talked to, more liable to roll at speeds of 50 mph and over than tender engines; equally it appeared that this did not only happen on curves, but also on straight sections where the road was not in sufficiently good order. In regard to the tendency of the K Class engines to roll, there had been continuous efforts to lessen it by successive alterations in the design.

As to the state of the track where the accident had happened, heavier loads were now being taken over it, and at higher speeds, than in the past. The specified amount of superelevation of the rail needed on the curve in question had not been correctly maintained, though in the opinions of the engineers and inspectors charged with its oversight it had not been dangerously incorrect and could not alone have explained the derailment. Markings on the rails and over the keys and chairs which supported them had shown clearly where the actual derailment had begun, and the extent to which the engine had rolled from side to side subsequent to the wheels leaving the track. These markings showed that the roll of the partly-derailed engine had increased in amplitude, indicating that once the the rollings had begun it increased rather than lessened; this may have been due to irregularity in the superelevation of the outer rail. The subsequent lessening of the period could well have been due to a lessening of the cant-irregularity, but might also have been the result of the closing of the regulator. Eventually the rolling had stopped – probably when the brake had been applied in the vinicity of the catch points, the bursting-open of which had caused the coaches behind the engine also to leave the rails.

A full examination of the damaged engine, made after it had been towed to Ashford Works, had shown that the wheels of the Bissel truck had not been the first to be derailed, and that its slides were in good condition and showed no sign of scoring. All the locomotive's wheels to the rear of the Bissel truck were correct to gauge and in good condition. The frames were very slightly out of square as a result of the impact they had received. The axleboxes appeared to have been moving freely in the horn guides. It clearly had been the leading coupled wheels which were the first to leave the track · a phenomenon which had occurred before with a large tank locomotive going at speed, on the LBSCR in 1914. Various other signs, markings and scratches on parts of the engine appeared to have been made subsequent to the derailment. All in all, there did not seem to have been anything about the locomotive which alone might have occasioned the accident.

It was otherwise in regard to the permanent way where the derailment had occurred. Here it seemed that the permanent way staff had failed to realise the extent to which the road had suffered under the heavy traffic that was passing over it, and in consequence of the wet weather.

The trials made of the two types of 2-6-4 tank locomotives on the LNER and SR main lines had borne out the statement of the former's Chief Mechanical Engineer that they were suitable for working express passenger trains on a well-maintained track, but also that they were sensitive to irregularities in the track because they were relatively lightly sprung and had side tanks which were wide apart, so that when they began to roll the amplitude of the latter was large, slow, difficult to damp out and likely to increase. If the speed were high the rolling might become dangerous, especially if some other movement in the engine were to synchronise with the period of the roll. Nevertheless, the fact that the engines had been used for a year and a half on express trains on the Central Section without derailment or complaint showed that it could hardly have been the easy springing of No. 800 which had been the main cause of its leaving the track, since Nos. 791 – 799, which had been used on that section, had even more resilient helical springs on their Bissel trucks and rear bogies than the engines of the later batch.

The fundamental cause of the accident had been the insufficiency of hard and clean ballast in the track for-

---

[1] These were timings of other typical high-speed services operated by tank engines on other lines, the numbers of such engines owned by the SR and other companies compared with their total locomotive stock, and the numbers of derailments of both tank and tender engines reported during the previous forty years.

[2] It is not clear why he thought the speed must have been so high. The evidence given by the driver and fireman of the derailed engine, by the signalmen in the boxes which it passed and the estimates of persons in the train all put the speed at not more than 60 mph.

mation, together with lack of proper drainage and irregularities in the level and gauge of the rails, so that serious rolling and lateral motion were imparted to tank engines travelling at high speed. The heavy rainfalls during the morning of 24th August might also have caused the track to go down rapidly under traffic, thus bringing about some of the irregularities afterwards observed.

'I find therefore' he wrote, 'that the condition of the road in respect of foundation and maintenance was the initial cause of rolling motion set up on Engine No. 800, which caused the derailment in the manner above described.'

He suggested that the following matters for the Company's attention:

1. The need to establish a better road bed and a higher quality of maintenance, since loads had increased and were being hauled by heavier engines at higher speeds.

2. Harsh springing on locomotives, though it might reduce some of the lateral movements to which engines were prone, caused rough riding and damage to the track and was in the long run uneconomical. (*He evidently had the 'King Arthurs' in mind, one of which had vibrated so badly during the trials.*)

3. Along important curves permanent pillars should be set up to show the extent of the cant required, and gangers should be issued with the appropriate tools for checking gauge and rail levels.

4. Permanent way officers and inspectors would do well to ride more frequently on locomotive footplates, which would inform them of the condition of the road bed and of the need for action.

5. In regard to the 'River' tanks, some limit of speed should be imposed wherever the permanent way was deficient in regard to type, drainage or maintenance. He also thought that the usual clearance between the

axleboxes and the hornstays might be increased, that a bogie truck might prove a better support for the front of the engine, that spring compensating levers might be employed, and that the question of whether engines of this Class should be fitted with tanks ought to be considered.

So far as the K Class locomotives were concerned, the Inquiry had immediate consequences; it was decided to rebuild them as tender engines. The first one to enter Ashford Works for this purpose actually did so before Sir John's report was **finally signed**. There had in fact been previous discussions about whether or not to multiply the Class, during which there had by no means been unanimity about the wisdom of doing so. Early in 1927 Maunsell had chaired meetings of the Locomotive Policy Committee, as a result of which it had been decided to construct twenty more 'Rivers', and names had actually been selected for them. But the discussions had shown up differences of opinion; members of the Locomotive Running Department had felt that there would not be enough duties available for them, as their water capacities were so limited, and that it would be better to build them as tender engines for working cross-country and semi-fast services. Consequently, though construction of the new engines was determined upon, work on them was deferred. Then came the Sevenoaks accident, and the Running Department was allowed to have its way; they were to be completed as tender engines. However, the 'River' tanks had received much adverse publicity, so it was later decided to omit the names. This was the origin of the U Class 2-6-0s, with 2 cylinders and 6 ft driving wheels.

Not un-naturally it was also decided to rebuild all the 2-cylinder Ks as Us with only slight differences from those which had already been ordered (the running plates being somewhat lower and the smokebox saddles somewhat larger). The first to emerge from Ashford

U class 2-6-0 No. A 792, formerly 'River Arun', soon after conversion. It has retained its piston tail rods, but these were eventually removed as being un-necessary.   *Courtesy: National Railway Museum Library*

Works in rebuilt form was No.A 805, in March 1928; the rest, except for the damaged engine No. A 800, were modified between June and August in the same year; finally No. A 800 took the road again in December. Those parts of the engines which had been removed – in particular the bunkers, side tanks and rear bogies - were put aside to be used again later; the following chapter describes how this was done. Many of these reconstructed engines were put into service before the first of the new ones emerged from Brighton works in August 1928; the last one of the new ones was not completed until May 1931.

No more fast passenger tank engines were built for the Southern Railway. Indeed, with one exception, mentioned below in Chapter 13, the same could be said in regard to the other railways in Great Britain, on which a number of Classes of 4-6-4 tanks, originally intended for the fastest passenger work, were still running, as well as those on the Central Section of the SR. These included the inside-cylindered 4-6-4s originally built for the Furness Railway, though of course on that line, between Carnforth and Whitehaven, high speeds were not possible. The Sevenoaks accident was probably a deciding factor in this general renunciation; many of them, too, had shown a propensity for rolling. Numbers of 2-6-4 tanks continued to be built, but only for suburban or freight work, though (as will be seen in chapter 13) some did run fast at times, When the SR returned to this wheel arrangement it was very definitely for non-passenger work only.

In regard to No. A 890, *River Frome*, which had shown itself to be a better engine than No. 803 in the Offord trials, it was rebuilt as the first of a new Class of 2-6-0s the 3-cylinder 'U1's. As such it left Ashford, with the same number but un-named, in June 1928. It retained the steep front leading down to the buffer beam, and also for a while retained the conjugated valve gear designed by Holcroft for operating the inside cylinder. It resembled the N1 3-cylinder 2-6-0 except in having larger driving wheels with splashers above the running boards. After it had been extensively tested for about a year, first between London and Hastings and then on the Portsmouth direct line from Waterloo and in the West of England, a further 20 were ordered. These latter were given rather larger tenders, since the prototype had been heavy in its consumption of water, though light on coal. They also had three independent sets of Walschaert's valve gear in place of the Holcroft conjugated system, since it had been found on the 'N1's that the advantages of the latter were cancelled out by the fact that its levers whipped at speed, so that the valve events inside the cylinder were not what they were in the other two. No. A 890 was also modified to resemble the others in 1932.

Both the 'U's and the 'U1's had reasonably long lives, and were all taken over by British Railways after distinguishing themselves in the Second World War by great feats of load haulage. On semi-fast and cross-country services, and on occasional summer Saturday expresses, they performed very creditably. Though officially limited to a maximum of 70 mph they often exceeded this in practice. In their later years they were given smoke deflectors and had the snifting valves removed from their smokeboxes. Four have been preserved.

Sir John Pringle's strictures on the permanent way and its inadequate maintenance were taken to heart, and the ballasting of the whole SR system was gradually improved, with supplies of granite chips from the Meldon quarries in Devonshire being brought in to replace the mixture of pebbles, ash, sand and ragstone previously used in Kent. The fact that the LSWR main line had been shown, in the second set of locomotive trials, to be in such a poor state was a humiliating eye-opener for the SR authorities, and particularly for the Chief Engineer, G Ellson; this fact, and the Sevenoaks derailment, seemed to have preyed on his mind and brought about a nervous breakdown which lasted for some months. It is a curious fact that the performance of the 'King Arthur' 4-6-0s, which when they first took the road had been generally poor, with time-keeping suffering in consequence, improved markedly at the end of the decade, and it may well have been that drivers were unwilling to let them show their paces because of the uncomfortable ride they gave them at speed over unsatisfactory portions of track. Eventually the main lines of the SR were made as good as any elsewhere in Great Britain, but by that time the Ks had all been transmogrified and the names they had borne had vanished into limbo.

U class 2-6-0 No. 1808 formerly 'River Char', heading a semi-fast train on the Eastern Section. Note the addition of smoke deflectors and the removal of the piston tail rods, which dates the photograph to some time in the middle or late thirties. *Courtesy: National Railway Museum Library*

12. USING UP THE BITS AND PIECES

From 1928 onwards no more six-coupled tank locomotives were built on the SR for fast passenger services. There were a few still in use on the Central Section - the two 4-6-2s built by Marsh and the seven 4-6-4s built by L. Billinton, and work was found for them for a while. One duty regularly allotted to a 4-6-4 was the haulage of the 'City Limited' daily from Brighton to London Bridge and back, a turn which could not be given to a 'King Arthur' because the turntable at London Bridge was not quite large enough. But once the extending electrification of the Southern system had reached the South coast there were no suitable duties left which they could perform as tank engines, so, like the 'K's, they were rebuilt with tenders to correspond with the 'King Arthur' in power, and were used on the Western Section.

However, Maunsell had kept the spare parts from the 'Rivers' in the expectation that sooner or later they could be used in a new design, and a special need soon arose for powerful freight engines in the London area. By 1930 almost the whole of the former LSWR, LBSCR and SECR network of lines South of the Thames as far as the North Downs had been electrified, and multiple-unit electric trains had replaced steam-hauled ones on the passenger services. Passenger train movements in this area were now brisker than before, with more rapid accelerations and decelerations between stations. Freight trains had to be correspondingly quicker at getting under way and slowing down, in order to fit in between electric trains without delaying them. Where lines had not been electrified, as in good yards and the spurs that led to and from them, gradients were in many places quite steep - in flyover junctions, for example. There was a good deal of freight traffic passing through and across South London. It could not match the electric trains in quick movement. 0-6-0 freight locomotives of the old kind, such as Wainwright's C Class, could cope with the trains of vans and wagons but could not accelerate quickly enough, nor stop fast enough, because of their limited braking power. A type of engine was needed capable of exerting a great force for a short time; sustained power output was not required since all the cross-London freight services were short-haul affairs. Steep gradients had to be easily surmounted, as in hump shunting yards. Braking had also to be efficient to enable quick stops with trains that did not have continuous brakes. A large number of such engines was not, however, needed since their sphere of work would be very restricted.

Maunsell solved this problem by designing a 2-6-4 tank engine which in general resembled the 3-cylinder 2-6-4 River Frome, though having smaller 5 ft 6 in driving wheels. The 3-cylinder arrangement was chosen to give the engine as even a starting torque as possible. Each cylinder had its own set of Walschaert's valve gear.

The boiler was interchangeable with those of the N, N1, U and U1 Classes; the cylinders, however, were half an inch greater in diameter than those of the other 3-cylinder engines, so that the nominal tractive effort was high as 29,376 lb. The side tanks, bunkers and rear bogies were those which had been removed from the 'K's and 'K1's when they were reconstructed, but there was a slight difference in the shape of the bunkers, the upper part of each being extended backwards for a few inches. They held 3½ tons of coal; the water capacity was 2,000 gallons, as with the Ks. Each engine was 2 tons heavier than the solitary K1 had been, and three-fifths of the weight was available for adhesion. Steam brakes were fitted, not only to the driving wheels but also to those of the rear bogie. While normally these engines would not be hauling continuously braked vehicles, this might occasionally happen, so that vacuum braking apparatus was also provided.

In external appearance they resembled River Frome but some differences were observable. The cab was given an extra window on each side. More of the coupled wheels were visible beneath the tanks, since they were smaller. The Holcroft conjugated gear rodding was missing. An extra pair of footsteps was provided, one on either side of the front buffer beam.

Five were built initially and ten more in 1935 – 1936. The earlier ones were liveried in black, with the green lining then usual on SR freight locomotives. The lettering and numbers were in yellow. The later ones were painted black without any lining, and when the first five came in for re-painting they were treated the same way. By this time, the Southern locomotives were being renumbered, so the A-prefix was removed and the number 1 added before the original number. After they had passed into the BR ownership a further figure 3 was prefixed.

The locomotives were very successful at their lowly job of short-distance freight haulage, and lasted until 1963 – 1964. When they were first built an absolute ban was placed on their working passenger vehicles, even empty stock, though the latter was eventually permitted. They were shedded at Stewart's Lane, Hither Green and Norwood Junction, and were continuously employed moving freight traffic handed over at Willesden or Old Oak from the LMS and GWR systems. Despite the hazards of wartime bombing they all escaped damage. After becoming part of BR stock one of them, No. 31918, was given a special test on passenger working between Victoria and Tunbridge Wells West, and kept time easily on a specially accelerated schedule. More impressively, a few days earlier it had been to Ashford to be prepared for these test runs and had hauled a six-coach train between Tonbridge and Ashford in 27 minutes 55 seconds; the return run took only 27 minutes with the same set of coaches. This was almost certainly the fastest running it or any of its sister-engines had ever been required to do, and a speed of at least 70 mph must have been attained at at least one point. The track was now of course in better shape than in the 'twenties, but there may well have been some on board the train who kept their fingers crossed and hoped history would not repeat itself.

Above: W class 2-6-4 No. 1911 soon after being built, posed in photographic grey, soon to be replaced by the black livery for all but express passenger locomotives. This and its fellows were designed to move goods trains in the London surburban area and accelerate rapidly enough not to delay the fast-moving electric trains. Parts previously taken from the rebuilt K tank engines were used in these engines, which much resembled the solitary K1 3-cylinder tank locomotive 'River Frome' in appearance, but had smaller wheels and lacked the Holcroft derived valve gear for the inside cylinder, which worked with an independent Walschaerts gear. *Courtesy: Kent County Library*

Below: W class 2-6-4 No. 31917 at Norwood Junction in BR days, 1956. Not in very clean condition, though the tank has been rubbed to display the BR 'Lion & Wheel' logo. *Courtesy: Photomatic Ltd*

13. COMMENTS AND CONCLUSIONS

A typical Icelandic saga relates the story of a remarkable man, usually a warrior of distinction, with a flaw, perhaps only a slight one, somewhere in his character, in consequence of which he is beset by circumstances in such a way as to make irreconcileable enemies and come to a violent end. After that the loose ends in the story are quickly tied up. The history of the 'River' Class resembles a saga, with the locomotive type as the tragic hero of the tale, and the chief villain (if that be the right metaphor) the unsatisfactory state of the track which caused it to suffer repeated accidents. The analogy, of course, is not perfect; to lose a bunker and side tanks and acquire a tender in their places is scarcely to be compared with a violent death, and perhaps if the locomotives had been allowed to keep their names one might have felt less regret; in that regard uninformed popular outcry may be cast in the role of a secondary villain. But if one is not to shed tears over the demise of a promising locomotive type, one may be pardoned a sigh or two, as one may for the dismantlement of Churchward's Pacific *The Great Bear* after a few years of insufficient use, or the scrapping of Bulleid's revolutionary 'Leader' 0-6-6-0.

When the 'Rivers' were first mooted and the prototype was constructed there seemed no reason why the SECR should not continue indefinitely as a successful going concern, and the standardisation policy of having only two new locomotive types, whose parts were nearly all interchangeable, which would by degrees take over most of the passenger and freight workings, made good sense, Maunsell and his team could reasonably assume that the road over which the engines were to run would be safe and suitable; the Engineer's department might be supposed to know its job as they knew theirs. Had there been no First World War, had the permanent way not been subjected for so long to all the strains and stresses of wartime traffic with a minimum of maintenance, the faults of the shingle-based track might well have been discovered and put right sooner, and the permanent way might have been raised to the level of quality which the LNER achieved thirty years after *it* had been in such a poor state that H.A. Ivatt, when he had taken up the post of Locomotive Superintendent, had declared he would never have done so if he had known the GNR track was in such a poor condition.

But there *was* a war, and the requirements of national defence took priority over everything else. This was especially so on the SECR. Ashford Works for a while became almost entirely an extension of the war effort. Then, as peace approached, followed the years of uncertainty, the Government vacillating between outright nationalisation of the whole railway system and its rationalisation into a few large private companies. With the coming of the Grouping in 1923 the whole landscape changed. What would have been a good and workable policy for the lines in the South-East of England alone was not applicable to the whole Southern system. There might be a place for tank engines working expresses on some parts of that railway – this was already being done on the Central Section – but not all over it. Meanwhile the prototype, No. 790, had been tested and found satisfactory in every respect except water capacity, which proved to be a little on the short side. No one complained that it rolled. It may well have been noticeably resilient on its springs. It was a feature of Maunsell's express engines that, as one SECR driver said, 'they would feel a fag card if they went over one', but complaints did not start to come in until the type had been multiplied.

Should this multiplication have been allowed to happen? It is easy to be wise after the event and say 'no'. When Maunsell and his team decided to build a further nine 2-6-0s their intended first sphere of work was not either of the main lines into Kent but the main Brighton line south of Victoria and London Bridge. Here seven large 4-6-4 tank engines, whose design was somewhat outmoded (they had not been built with one eye on what Swindon was doing) were hauling the prestige trains. A locomotive of comparable power but many tons lighter would surely be an improvement. So nine new 'Rivers' were introduced, and the prototype joined them. They showed that they were as good as the 4-6-4s in test runs and in daily service. As to their steadiness, there is some conflict of opinion. In his book *The Locomotives of the South Eastern & Chatham Railway* D.L. Bradley, writing in 1961, says that the Central Section footplate crews 'did not appreciate their marked tendency to roll heavily and unexpectedly on indifferent track, and consequently refused to run them at high speeds.' He goes on to imply that because of this tendency they had by Easter 1927 mostly been moved to Eastern Section sheds. One wonders if he had been conversing with former drivers long after the event, after the Sevenoaks accident, when they had been widely stigmatised as not merely given to rolling, but to rolling unsafely. The fact remains that no written complaints were about the prototype and its nine immediate successors, that they rolled at speed, until they had all been taken off the chief express duties on the Central Section when the 'King Arthur' 4-6-0s with 6-wheeled tenders were introduced. Nine of these ten engines, too, were the unmodified ones with helical wheel springs, not the later ones which had been given laminated springs to make them steadier. It was of the latter that complaints were made when they rode on the Eastern Section, and it was two of these which suffered derailment. It was almost as if the alterations intended to make them steadier had had the opposite effect.

At any rate, the second batch of engines was built, and two of them were assessed by H.N. Gresley and given a clean bill of health; on well-maintained track, he declared, they could safely be driven at any speed they were capable of attaining. But after Sevenoaks, and the unfavourable publicity which followed it, the dog had been given a bad name and had to be hung. Could this have been avoided? Probably it could if the permanent way had been put into a satisfactory state in a very short while. But that was not possible; it was bound to be a matter of years rather than months. The Meldon granite quarries were far away, and the number of men available to do the repairs was limited. It was necessarily a long job. Reluctantly, therefore, one has to agree that the right decision was made when the entire class was ordered to be converted to tender engines. As such they gave good service, and had the additional advantage that they were not liable to run short of water. They also stopped rolling. But it was a pity that they could not retain their names.

The Sevenoaks accident marked the end of the policy of building large six-coupled tank engines for work on fast trains. However, it cannot be said that practice invariably followed policy. In 1927 Sir Henry Fowler, Chief Mechanical Engineer of the LMSR, was about to produce a 2-6-4 tank engine for general purposes, suitable for use on all parts of the system. In dimensions it was not greatly dis-similar from the K tanks, with two outside cylinders, Walschaert's valve gear, coupled wheels 5 ft 9 in diameter, the same boiler pressure and a similar water capacity. Following the accident, Fowler contacted Sir John Pringle to seek his opinion on the new design, and was told it was unobjectionable provided no attempts were made to run it at high speed. So building went ahead and as many as 125 were constructed at Derby during 1927 – 1934. It was not indeed designed for fast running, but with a good front-end arrangement it did in fact run fast on many occasions when used in the London outer suburban services; admittedly this happened on well-maintained roads. Timings inwards to St. Pancras from St. Albans of 25 minutes (19.9 miles) and from Watford to Euston in 22 minutes (17.4 miles) provided the opportunity, if time had to be made up, of running light suburban trains at 80 miles an hour and more on downhill stretches, and drivers frequently took advantage of the free-running abilities of these engines. Nothing untoward ever occurred - which suggests that had the track been as good on the SR the Ks might have worked on their days happily enough on the line for which they were intended.

The 'Rivers', so far as the writer is aware, were the only complete locomotive Class to suffer entire obliteration following a mishap to one of their number. Had the Sevenoaks accident occurred forty years earlier the consequences might have been different. The engine type had been freed from sole blame; it might have continued to be used, a few precautions being taken. This happened with Patrick Stirling's final batch of single wheeler 8-footers. Two of these were involved in accidents at speed, with loss of life, and there is a strong suspicion that undue weight on the driving wheels was a contributory cause. But they were not taken off the road, though alterations were made to the distribution of weight on their wheels. No one, so far as we know, felt apprehensive when he saw one of Stirling's last half-dozen backing on to his train at Kings Cross. But the popular press did not then exist as it existed in the 'twenties. The GNR, too, was a popular line, where as in 1927 the Southern was still living down a reputation for slowness and unpunctuality which was largely due to the greater involvement of its constituent lines in the war effort, which had caused its track to deteriorate more thoroughly than that of other lines which had not been used so intensively to carry troops and munitions. Then, as now, some newspaper proprietors and editors were more concerned to sell their papers by sensational and slanted reporting than to be truthful and fair. In those days, too, they formed public opinion more than now. So perhaps it may be said that the 'Rivers' were sacrificed on the altar of a wrongly-informed public opinion, like the famous Admiral Byng, who was shot on his own quarter-deck by orders of the Admiralty *pourencourager les autres*, as Voltaire ironically put it.

Details and Dimensions of Maunsell's 2-6-4 tank engines:

Class:	K	K.1	W
Length of Boiler:	12 ft 6 in	12 ft 6 in	12 ft 6 in
Diameter of Boiler at smokebox:	4 ft 7 ¾ in	4 ft 7 ¾ in	4 ft 7 ¾ in
Diameter of Boiler at Firebox:	5 ft 3 in	5 ft 3 in	5 ft 3 in
Heating Surface (sq. ft):	1,525	1,525	1,728
Superheater surface (sq. ft):	203*	203*	285
Grate area (sq. ft):	25	25	25
Boiler pressure (lb./sq. in):	200	200	200
Number of cylinders:	2	3	3
Cylinders: dia. & length (ins):	19 x 28	16 x 28	16 ½ x 28
Diameter of coupled wheels:	6 ft	6 ft	5 ft 6 in
Diameter of truck & bogie wheels:	3 ft 1 in	3 ft 1 in	3 ft 1 in
Total weight in working order (tons):	82.6	88.75	90.75
Coal capacity (tons)	2 ½	2 ½	3 ½
Water capacity (gallons):	2,000	2,000	2,000
Tractive effort (lb).			
at 85% of boiler pressure:	23,870	25,390	29,380

* Later increased to 285.